D0805209

DEAR SELF

*This is Me Being There for You
When You Need Me the Most.*

ruby dhal

Ruby Dhal

Written and arranged by Ruby Dhal

Piction Books Ltd

Other poetry/prose books by Ruby

Memories Unwound	(2017)
A Handful of Stars	(2018)
My Hope for Tomorrow	(2019)
Herinneringen Ontward	(2019)
Handvol Sterren	(2020)

Personal Note.

This book is different from the others. And if you're like me and like to jump straight to the last page of a book to get a sense of what the story holds – it's a bad habit, but I do it anyway – you've probably already figured this out. This book conveys a narrative. One where I speak directly to you all. I express my emotions with utmost clarity. I'm as honest and raw as I can be. And most importantly, I delve into my yesteryears to finds jewels of wisdom that can help you as much as they helped me.

More writing means more vulnerability. It means that people will find out stuff about me that they didn't know before. Stories that I've hidden in the folds of my heart. Episodes in my life that I don't speak about openly. It means turning back and diving into the past to move into the future.

I talk about a few chapters in my life to point out several truths, and these are as follows:

a. I'm imperfect
b. We all make mistakes
c. I've learned from my past; therefore, I know what I'm talking about (kind of)
d. Like you, I'm still learning

Most of the time, I don't mind being vulnerable.

Being vulnerable means shedding my regrets and planting the seeds of teachings for myself and you. It means recognising my insecurities and flaws to enable you to do the same. Being vulnerable means that other people (those whom I haven't known for a long time and don't share a close relationship with) will learn a lot more about my personal life. A lot more than I would like them to know.

As vocal as I am about the topics that I share online – I'm a very private person. Most people aren't aware of what I've undergone, or how much. This book means that you will find out a lot more about me than I normally share. That's fine with me. Because if I'm able to highlight an invaluable message through my vulnerabilities, then I don't mind being this open.

I want to light up the truth that being vulnerable doesn't mean being weak. Transparency isn't necessarily bad.

But being honest about your experiences sometimes means making other people vulnerable too. That's the part that I'm struggling with. I'm okay with talking about my experiences if they were *only my experiences to talk about*. But like everything else, my past involves other people and the stories I tell may make those people feel exposed.

Sometimes, the lessons, difficulties and regrets that you carry on your back are heavy with memories of your time with others. On this occasion, I would like to apologise in advance for being honest. My honesty may upset those who've been a part of my past. Some may read this book and get upset that I've spoken about them in this way. They might assume that I'm telling one side of a whole truth that involves their perspective too.

I want to clarify this to every person who has played a part in my growth – I'm not trying to prove that I was right. All I'm doing is talking about my insight from those events and how I turned those weaknesses into strengths that bettered my life.

You may have been right in your place, but I was also right in mine.

Sometimes, what's wrong is the circumstances that you find yourself in, not the people that those circumstances put you against. What I want to do with this book is underline that our perspectives differ, and this is what guides us in taking positive steps towards self-discovery. My perspective is written in this book. It explains why I acted the way that I did. My perspective allowed me to take invaluable wisdom from those situations. My perspective is mine only, but it doesn't exist to devalue someone else's perspective.

To my friends and family that read these stories – please read them with a pinch of salt. I don't hold any grudges or darkness in my heart. All I hold is the memories and learning.

To my readers – please understand that life goes on without you. Life doesn't wait for you to get your act together, tapping its index finger against an invisible watch wrapped around its imaginary wrist, to indicate that you're running out of time. Life moves forward. And if you're sitting there, moping around about all that you did wrong and all the wounds you made in other people's hearts as you were growing – you will never be able to move on.

You need to look at your reflection in the mirror, wipe off the past from your forehead and let yourself start again.

The aim of this book is to guide you in grasping that you're only human, so stop being hard on yourself. I want to point you in the direction of flourishing, purpose and healing.

I hope that after hearing my story, you will be easier on yourself with yours.

Self-Love/ Self-Worth

The beauty of loving yourself – self-love and self-worth.

A lot of my pieces are about self-love and self-worth. Adopting these two in my life have caused a tumultuous stir in my healing journey, one that allowed me to reach a place of light sooner. Without embracing the truth that self-love is the antidote to a lot of the heartache that we undergo – I wouldn't be where I am today.

Think about it. If we loved ourselves then we wouldn't let people treat us poorly. We wouldn't allow them to get away with saying unkind words or acting against our welfare – when we would never do that to them. We wouldn't accept weak justifications for toxic behaviour. We wouldn't even tolerate toxic behaviour to begin with if we loved ourselves.

If we loved ourselves then we wouldn't say, *'It's okay'*, the first, second and third time that they screwed up. We wouldn't sit facing them, our eyebrows scrunched together in a sad frown, our elbows resting on the hard, wooden table with our chins propped on top as we wait for another, *'I'm sorry. I promise that I'll treat you better.'* And as those words tumbled out of their mouth, our stomach would descend like a packed elevator, because we'd know that those words are what they appear to be – mere words. Because positive actions would never follow.

If we loved ourselves, then we wouldn't settle for less than what we deserve. Heck, we wouldn't let it near us. We would wear our self-worth like a crown on our head, displaying the high regard with which we'd view ourselves and anyone who would come along, offering less than what our crown symbolises – we would zap them from our lives instantly.

Self-love steers us away from people that aren't good for us. It stops us from spreading our arms out to let in bad behaviour, negative vibes or actions that reduce our self-worth/actions that don't respect us. Self-love stops us from allowing empty promises, half-hearted love and the kind of pain that we could have avoided if we had prioritised ourselves.

Repeat after me: *I will put myself first.*

Love yourself enough to know when to stomp your foot down and assert, *'I'm not going to take it anymore'.* Love yourself enough to recognise negative vibes, toxicity and actions that may cause you discomfort. Love yourself enough to say *'no'*, not once or twice, but time and time again when your wellbeing requires it of you. Love yourself enough to never let someone else eat into your happiness or peace. Love yourself enough to put yourself before people who have no interest in caring for you.

Let self-love and your self-worth guide you. Embrace your inherent worth and love yourself with every fibre of your being. Only then will you make the most of your life and welcome happiness that will rattle in your core. Only then will you stretch your arms out, tilt your head back and breathe in the soft air, silken with calm. Only then will you feel a sliver of joy run through your spine whenever you wake up to greet the morning, looking forward to what the day holds.

Only then will you appreciate the swell of love that comes from people who are unafraid to tell you that they want you, people whose actions fall in line with their words, people who respect you more than you've ever known, people who bring out the best in you. Only then will you let those people grip your hand tight when you're overwhelmed, or when fear hangs heavy in the air and you don't know which way to go. Only then will you thread your fingers through theirs and clench them tightly, letting your body churn with comfort and ease. Letting yourself fall in love with life all over again.

Let self-love and self-worth guide you.

Only then will you stop settling for less and hold on to all that is right for you tightly against your chest.

Acceptance

I want to look at my reflection in the mirror and, for once, embrace the face staring back at me. I want to be proud of my eyes, my nose, and my lips, and the generous curves that God has given me without feeling guilty. Without scrutinising myself for not living up to the unrealistic beauty standards that society has painted. It's difficult. It's a struggle. I tell myself that this body is a gift and I should appreciate it as much as I can, that I should cradle my scars and believe that they truly make me glow. But it's hard loving yourself in a world that constantly reminds you how imperfect you are. How fragile you are. How small you are compared to everyone else.

I want to absorb myself entirely, but I know that it is a battle that I will lose 10 times before I win on the 11th.

But I will not give up.

Even when I'm given more reasons not to love myself. Even when I'm reminded that my tummy is threefold and my lips too thin, and of the lines that wrinkle up at the corner of my eyes whenever I smile, and my puffy cheeks and pointy chin – I won't forget the heart that's within it all. I'll appreciate how beautiful I am, both on the inside and out. I'll acknowledge that all those features make me glow more than I've ever known. I won't forget what makes me unique. And I won't forget what I'm worthy of. I will keep working on myself. I will keep striving. And when I look at my reflection in the mirror – *I will embrace myself completely.* In my entirety. Exactly how I should.

Happiness

It is hard. When you've known pain for too long, it's hard to believe that happiness belongs with you. It's even harder to squeeze happiness without the nagging thought at the back of your mind, telling you that it won't stay for too long because it's a visitor that's settled on the couch in the bright side of your room, closest to the door – ready to leave again. It's hard pushing away the fear that one day happiness will get up and head towards that same door. One day happiness will switch the lights off and leave you alone with the bleakness of your fluttering thoughts once more.

When you've been conditioned to group love with pain – you start to think that this is all that love can offer you. You presume that this is all that life can offer you. That's why it is important to welcome change. It's vital to witness new shades of life and let people teach us that love can be fuzzy, warm and good for your soul, and happiness doesn't always come with the fear that it will leave.

Sometimes it comes with the promise that it will stay.

All you need to do is welcome it with open arms and a heart spread wide enough to let it stay, wide enough to let in people, and adventures in new countries where the wind flows in a different direction and the mountains peak higher than the clouds, so you start to grasp that the sky isn't the limit, because the sun and stars are.

No one can stop you from reaching new heights if you have

faith in yourself.

Happiness, love and everyone who is kind to you belongs with you, and even if yesterday was difficult and today is a little hard – tomorrow will always bring with it the potential for a new start, for new beginnings, for the sun, the rain and rainbows that will wash away all the pain and tears. It will bring with it hope. Positivity. It will bring with it everything that you never imagined you would find.

Trust me, because it will.

Your Worth

Listen to me clearly – you are worthy. In every single way.

With your darkness, your light and your messy parts. With your insecurities and your discomfort. You are worthy of the love that you wished for yourself but haven't seen a glimpse of in a while because life has been difficult for you. You are worthy of the care and affection that you give to others.

You love more than they do, and this is why you hurt more. It's the truth. Being the one with the broader heart – without a cap – means that others are easily able to reach within and take what you have to offer without returning a fraction of it.

You are worthy because you treat people with affection, care and bucketloads of respect. You are worthy because you want there to be light for everyone, even if you don't have confidence that it will exist for you. You are worthy, even when you don't believe that you are. Even if, these days everywhere you turn, life hits you like a brick wall.

One bad day doesn't mean anything. It's only a small droplet in the wide expanse of life that you have left before you. Unkind words don't have the power to tarnish you, especially when you don't let them get to you. I know how hard it is to develop thick skin and to find strength in being soft. It's difficult not to let stuff get to your heart. It's difficult denying the niggling thought that *the horrible way people treat you is proof that you don't deserve love.* It's difficult to reject criticism, but it isn't impossible. Especially when you realise that bitter words and ill-treatment reflects their self-esteem – not yours.

Often, people treat us badly without a reason because they're dealing with their own battles. Perhaps your existence/ appearance makes it worse for them to come to terms with their existential crisis. For this reason, they put you down. They treat you badly.

None of this justifies their behaviour. If they treat you horribly then you need to cut them off. But what it does mean is that *you are worthy*, regardless of what they say and how they treat you. Their opinion of you doesn't define you. Their refusal to love you back doesn't define you. Their rejection of you doesn't define you. *They don't define you.*

Listen to me clearly – *you are worthy*. In every single way. Including all your highs and lows. Including the old friendships and lost lovers. Including every rejection and failure. Including every low period in your life. You are worthy and you will continue to be worthy.

Regardless of what others say.

Regardless of what they feel.

Regardless of what they do.

Find Yourself

Find yourself in your soft reflection in the mirror. Find yourself in the streak of sunlight that sneaks in through the thin gaps between your blinds, and in the way you smile when it traces the lines across your lips, your face, and settles on your closed eyelids, welcoming you to a new morning. Find yourself in the conversations with your friends, where you bounce from coffee, to lunch, to the way you felt when you sunk your feet into the white sand beach of a foreign country thousands of miles from home, and how it would feel to stand under the Sistine chapel, pushing your head back and glancing up at a ceiling bathed in art and history that existed thousands of years before you.

Find yourself in uncertainty, in not knowing where you're headed but with the desire to take adventures along the way. Find yourself in taking risks, in giving up, letting go and starting all over again. Find yourself in welcoming growth and being humble. Find yourself in being kind.

Find yourself in cafés tucked away in the pleats of busy streets with the rain pounding on the windowsill while you get cosy inside, reading your favourite book, lit up by the mustard glow of fairy lights hanging overhead. Find yourself in laughter, tears and how the years wear on – turning happy moments into memories that warm you up when you recall them. Find yourself in books, stories, and songs that pull you back through a tornado of the past.

Find yourself in love, and in your lover. Find yourself in the twinkle of their eyes when they gaze at you and in the glow that settles deep on their face. Find yourself in their embrace, in the softness of their hands that caress your face and in their heart-warming chuckle. Find yourself in the truth that your smile doesn't leave for hours even after they do. Find yourself in their voice that always roots for you, in their mind that scurries with images of you, in their soul that has found a home with yours and in their heart, which beats undeniably for you.

Find yourself in joy, tears and everything in between. Find yourself in the way the sun sets, and the clouds ascend. Find yourself in the truth that love can break you, but true love gives you life. Find yourself in each step that you take towards what is truly meant for you. Keep finding yourself. Even when you assume that you've found what you were looking for – keep searching. Because there is always room to learn and there is always room to grow. As you walk on this beautiful journey called life, you will find so much more than you ever thought you would.

What does 'find yourself' truly mean?

Let me be honest. Sometimes I sound like a schoolteacher.

I advise you all to *'be happy'*, *'be brave'* and *'love yourself'*, as if I'm writing out these rules on a squeaky chalkboard, expecting you to copy them down. Expecting you to follow them like the golden rules of a classroom. I know how it feels. You're overwhelmed by all that you've endured so far, wondering how you will come through from it. Then a word, sentence or story flash before your eyes; something that's relatable – pulling you in. Getting your attention. Stringing you along to finish reading until you reach the end and think, *'Wait, how am I supposed to get there?'*

Because the words are all correct. They make sense. The sentence that you're reading talks knowledgeably about your current life situation. It affirms your need to heal. Your desire to be happy again. Your decision to move on. But how do you get to this place that this speaker, coach or writer creates? You've been given the measurement of each ingredient required to bake a cake, without the apparatus or the recipe. You're wondering – *'Yes, I would like to remove toxic people from my life. I want to reach a place of contentment. I want my mindset to be positive.'*

But what actions do you need to take to do this? What path do you need to choose?

Because it all sounds great, but when it comes down to taking the journey there – the road is ambiguous and staggering.

That's the difficult part, because every person is different.

What I try to do with my pieces is to shed light on where the emotions that you desire the most can be found. For instance, if I speak about happiness and advise that you embrace it, I refer to the possibility increasing interactions that can make you happy. I talk about partaking in activities that might excite you or returning to old routines that used to bring you joy in the past. It's not possible for me to *specify exactly what you need to do* in order to reach a state of happiness, because joy is perceived differently by everyone. But I can outline what *being active* in your life to bring about that happiness looks like. I can stress the importance spending time with new people and old friends or going out of your way to enjoy the company of those who have the potential to bring you undoubted joy.

Happiness, just like sadness, peace and love etc. looks different for every person. What I can do is emphasise how vital it is to be active in your journey to make the most of those emotional states, but it's up to you to find the path that takes you there. I give you the ingredients, but you decide what apparatus you want to use. You create the recipe from scratch – or by using mine as a guide.

In relation to the piece above, titled *'Find Yourself'*, what my piece insinuates is that you can find an essence of yourself by participating in a variety of experiences. Such as adventures, meeting people, trying something new, facing your challenges, investing precious time in being alone, waking up with a positive mindset into new mornings and making the most of blissful nights.

That's a lot to do – isn't it?

It really isn't.

Consider it this way. You take part in so many activities each day without giving it a second thought. You wake up either in a positive or negative mood – this depends on the quality of your sleep and your evening routine, but we won't go into too much detail in relation to that. You have breakfast. Then you delve into your morning routine – jogging, reading, watching TV, listening to music, meditating or doing nothing. Most of us skip that part on weekdays and rush to work. You speak with your colleagues and managers at work. You take a break and go to lunch and perhaps meet up with a friend. Maybe you go shopping during your lunch break instead. Then you take public transport or drive home. Perhaps you go to the gym after that or an evening walk. No, it's date night today. Or a party.

You know what? You would rather spend your evening unwinding at home.

Whatever it is, you have a routine in place which involve innumerable interactions with the outside world, as well as yourself. These interactions make up your day, week, month and year. But have you ever thought about what these encounters are doing for you?

Are they making you sad?

Are they bringing you down?

Do the people whom you spend the most amount of time with contribute to your wellbeing?

To find yourself, then – your deepest, truest self – would mean having more exchanges that *promote soul-searching and allow you to appreciate more joy in your life.* This involves experiences that encourage a realisation of your identity and enhance the positivity that currently exists in your life.

Sure, you can't get rid of your workday, an annoying neighbour, or the colleague who keeps rabbiting away about a mole on their butt. But what you can do this – you can choose to do more of what makes you happy. You can choose to look for a new job if your current one makes you unhappy. You can choose to meet up with your best friend for lunch. You can call your mother after work. You can go to the gym if it clears your mind. You can take a walk by yourself to the park. You can read, cook, watch Netflix or chill. Or you can dance your night away at your favourite club. You can make more plans with your friends and family – if that's what brings you joy.

The choice is yours only.

But, what does *find yourself* mean on these occasions? What are we looking for and what will we find in the end?

When I write pieces about self-discovery and self-worth, I have the following line of thought – when we start these journeys, we've lost something. To some degree, at least. I admit that not everyone is broken. But there are those of us who are. Not everyone has lost themselves through circumstances. But some of us have. That is what I want you to find. But remember, you're not only finding what you've lost – but so much more than that.

The truth is – as much as you would like to go back to the person you were before the loss, you can't. It's not possible. Going back would mean stripping off months and years from your life. It would mean relinquishing all the good times as well as the bad. It would mean rendering all the wisdom that came from those events non-existent.

There is no going back – *all you can do is go forward*. This means that when you're finding yourself after losing yourself, you're not finding the old you but are developing a new you. This isn't a bad thing.

For example, one fine day you decide to boil a jug of water for a few minutes before letting it cool outside. After cooling it, you put it into the freezer, and it forms into ice. Following that, you remove the ice from the freezer to let it melt once more. After it has melted, the water reaches the same temperature that it was before you boiled it, let it cool, froze it and melted it. However, this water isn't the same. It may look the same –

albeit less in volume. It may taste the same too. But it's different. The mineral content of water fluctuates/is lost in this process of *changing states*, even though the water looks the same by the end. After boiling, cooling, freezing and melting – the water particles have changed, been broken and moulded into something new. Into something different.

That's exactly how we – as humans – are.

Experiences burn us, cool us down and harden us until we melt into who we were always meant to be. This means that you're never going to mould into the same person again. Because you're not that person anymore. Instead, you will mould into someone new. Into the person you were always supposed to be. There's a huge difference between who you were and who you become because of the depth of your experiences that fill that space in between. The purpose isn't to return to the person you once were – but to sculpt yourself into a new person.

Your essence remains, but through the process of hurting, learning, and healing – you adopt numerous life skills. A new perspective. Strength. A purpose. You adopt more than you ever had before.

This is what I want you to find as you surge forward in the rollercoaster that is life.

The *'process of finding'* is ambiguous.

I can't show you exactly what you need to do to find yourself. What I can do is highlight my own progress and how I found myself. The reason for this is as follows – each one of us has a very particular, unique journey. Our childhood, the relationships that we witness between our parents, the attachments we form and everything that we undertake before a certain age controls a huge chunk of who we become later. All those events have a significant impact on our susceptibility to pain, heartache, love, failure etc. From this, the interactions that we have later in our lives shape our worldview and determine our coping mechanisms towards each hurdle that we face. We don't respond in the same way to challenges. Love. Failure. Success. Loss. Grief. Friendships. We don't respond in the same way when our lives are mending either. That's the beauty of being the individuals that we are.

We are profoundly different.

What unites us is the truth that we feel emotions in a similar way. Meaning, the physiological and psychological effect that those emotions have on us is – more or less – the same. It's for this reason that we can relate to each other in several matters. This makes it convenient to talk about one person's experience to shed light on how another person can deal with theirs.

What I've witnessed can't determine what will make you happy/sad. It can't tell you what will heal your heart, or what you need to do to find yourself. But what it can do is this – it can shed light on what *it looks like* to find yourself. It can encourage you to explore your mind and heart to uncover what peace means to you, what finding yourself entails and, perhaps, what to expect on your healing journey.

This is how I want you to approach your journey to self-discovery.

Draw light from other people's practices. Observe what they did, how they faced challenges and what skills they developed and apply it to your own life. Look at the scattered ingredients required for your healing and create your own recipe for love. For finding yourself. For adventuring and undertaking all the other wonderful expeditions that cultivate your life.

I can't produce a universal recipe for the challenges that you face in life. But what I can do is lay out the ingredients that I needed to brew the *'potion'* that worked on my life. I can draw examples from the actions that worked for me to point out what might work for you. And, trust me, when you use my recipe on your life, it will naturally change and give value to your life episodes.

It will become the recipe that you need.

It will become *your healing recipe* – encompassing everything that you need to bake that perfect cake.

The time I found myself after finding friends.

The first time I acknowledged that I was finding myself was after I made some friends – four of them, to be precise. These individuals had no idea who I was before my 21 years. They hadn't seen me at my lowest but were about to meet me at – and contribute to – my best. I found three of them while I was working part-time at Next (a clothing retail store here in the UK). I made the fourth friend outside work.

By the time I met them, 1 year had passed since my initial heartbreak. I was mending. I was in a better place both mentally and emotionally. I was writing and working towards my first book. Words like *'self-love'* and *'acceptance'* were stringing into my daily vocabulary and I was slowly affirming myself, even after struggling with it for innumerable years before that. Overall, *I was happy*, but I knew that I had the potential to be happier. The reason I say this is because, some nights I would still stay wide awake for a long time with questions circling my brain. Questions that I still had no answers for. When I smiled, my cheeks pulled back and I felt a genuine rush of warmth in my heart, but those same emotions would flee my body when I was alone, making it a cage of emptiness once more.

It was a difficult period in my healing. One where I was enjoying myself but also twisting my head back to look into the past. My eyes would still bundle with sadness when I recalled the lowest point in my life, and I would have to gulp down a rush of tears that threatened to overwhelm me. I was a lot stronger. I was getting there. But I wasn't there yet.

It was during this period that my four friends arrived in my life.

They came in my life out of the blue. The first three I'd been working with for a few months, but we didn't become good friends until we did some early morning shifts together, and the last one was someone I was following on social media for a long time before we stumbled across each other over an Instagram post.

All four of these friends had varying personalities. Two of them brought out the adventurous, fun-loving side of me – together we were the *three musketeers*. The third one was silly and a joy to talk to, and we had a similar worldview on many topics. The last one was the closest to my soul. We had heart-to-hearts during our Sunday shifts at work. I could go to her for every big/small problem in my life and would come out either with a definite answer to my problem or a direction to go in.

These four individuals were the bane of my happiness for two years. We would laugh, have meaningful conversations and some of the craziest moments together which strengthened our friendship over time. Before I knew it, these people became an integral part of my life. Not a day would pass where we wouldn't speak, and they brought immeasurable positivity and light into my life. I smiled and laughed more. I headed into each new morning with a fresh perspective. I looked forward to the day – I had not done this for a long while prior to that.

Before them, I had several friends. Friends that were a laugh to be around. Friends that were there for me when I needed them. But none of them were like these four individuals. The four friends that I'd now made had created a pedestal for the positive energy that I needed in my life. Two of these friends were boys and they contributed significantly to my re-evaluation of my 'ideal partner'. The more that I conversed with these two, the deeper my perception was of what a healthy relationship looks like.

They treated me respectfully. With care. They understood my dreams. They made me laugh. They brought me joy. They valued my presence and most importantly – they accepted me.

The last one is incredibly important to me. *Acceptance.*

I spent years before these individuals – doubting my existence. I believed that I wasn't deserving of love, or that I had to try my best to earn it. I had experienced too much. My childhood and adolescent years made it difficult for me to absorb the reality that love was a choice, it was an action, not a reward only given to those deemed special. When I'd walk into a room brimming with people that I knew, I would dwindle. I felt insignificant. My insecurities would choke me with despair.

I felt like an outsider.

Eventually I understood that these thoughts were just my demons eating at my resolve, and it took a lot more than making new friends for me to love myself wholeheartedly. And I've spent my entire life peeling off those doubts and uncertainties.

But when these wonderful souls came along in my life, without an inkling of what I had been through, they created a safe space for me where I felt understood and welcomed, and they didn't even know it. Perhaps they were aware of what I had witnessed in my years prior to them. Maybe they had the relevant connections and prying mind to find out the truth before it would ever tumble out of my mouth. But that didn't matter. What mattered was that my friends valued me in as a significant person in their life for *who I was now* and *who I would become* – not who I had been.

For people who carry a staggering amount of baggage like me – this level of regard is incredible.

My friends affirmed my worth. They understood my passion. They valued my presence and cherished my existence. I know what's going through your mind, *'Ruby, you shouldn't rely on other people to affirm or validate your existence'*, and I'm the biggest advocate for this. But suppose that you're in a deep, dark pit, diminishing under low self-esteem. You've been rejected and devalued time and time again by those you cared about. You were left behind by friends whom you'd known your whole life, despite them promising you that they would always be there for you.

You feel useless. Confused. And unsure about your place in the world. You don't know what's wrong with you, and you start to believe that you will ever come through from this. In this state of mind, nothing your alter ego says to you is acknowledged by you. You're anxious and you can't come out from it. Even though to the world you look fine – you are broken on the inside. You try your best but you're still unable to pull yourself together and move forward.

When you're in this place, the care and compassion of other people makes a huge difference. Something as tiny as, 'I appreciate you', or 'You are deserving', can give you the courage that you need to face one more day, to fight one last battle.

It's for this reason that no matter how much I say that you don't need other people to validate you – sometimes, when you're in an unsteady place, other people can pour their love into you. They can provide you with the courage that you need to get up once more. They can wrap you up in warmth and help you move on from this difficult phase in your life. Other people can't validate you but they can support you in finding your way out of that deep hole so you can start validating yourself.

This doesn't mean that you need to rely on other people forever in your journey. Normally, when you're feeling as low as I described, the gentleness of others can soften the blow in the initial period after the event. Following this, you will do fine on your own. But when you're at your lowest – other people's love and concern can do wonders for your healing.

I was fine before these friends came along. Even if they didn't bring positivity into my life, or the confidence that I developed, I would've discovered it if I came across a few more people who were their polar opposite (because them treating me badly would also impart a vital lesson), or if I continued to work on myself over time. But they sped the process of me finding myself, and I'm truly grateful to them for this. As our friendship matured, a sense of happiness enveloped every angle of my life. I started looking forward to life, even if it was filled with hardships because I was prepared to face them. Whenever I told my reflection in the mirror that I was deserving – I truly felt it.

My friends didn't do anything out of the ordinary. They were generous souls who only knew how to spread light and good vibes. And slowly, but surely, I began rebuilding myself considerably. I uncovered new shades of joy. Shades that made my life brighter. Shades that dragged all the darkness out and trickled it with a soft hue.

If you have people in your life who bring you this much joy – you naturally find parts of yourself that were hidden away. Parts that have faith in you. Parts that want you to flourish. Parts that love every particle of your existence. Parts that know you are worthy. You don't recall how, when, or where – but you fall in love with yourself in ways you never imagined.

Bright souls are hard to find.

You're more likely to find people who bring you down with them, belittle your dreams and question everything about you.

Trust me, I've been there. I spent years detangling myself from knots of friendships that I never wanted to get into to begin with. But still, years later I was buried, chest deep, in a swamp of toxic situations that I could've avoided if I had listened to the voice inside my head that blared at me from the start. The voice that echoed in my mind when I first met these people, telling me that they weren't going to benefit my life in any way.

The purpose of this example is to point out how important the people that you surround yourself with are. Because it was during this time that I made four genuine friends who had a tremendous impact on my life. They made a space for themselves in my heart that no one else can take. I didn't know these people before my heartbreak, but once I got to know them; everything about my heartbreak became a detached memory that wasn't able to cause me a single spike of pain anymore.

A healing journey, when taken alone, can get very lonely.

It's difficult when you open your eyes to light cracking through your curtains, with only darkness settled within you. Because even as the day passes, the light won't shine through you until you make space for it – until you remove the darkness. Healing is softer when you open your eyes, and heart, to people who shine with light, because theirs is easier to get through. The kind of light that doesn't care whether there is darkness inside you because it will shine through you anyway.

The right people quell the ache in your heart without realising it. The right people have faith in you, pushing you to have faith in yourself and love yourself more and more each day. The right people bring a storm of sunshine, love and laughter into your life. The right people cause your heart to clatter with happiness. The right people bring you courage.

Healing is inevitable.

The characteristic power of time will ensure that your heart mends itself slowly, yet surely. But with the right people in your life, healing becomes an adventure that you take with the people that you love the most – an adventure that no one wants to go on alone. Because life, in all its chaos – is a lot more fun with others by your side.

Find yourself. Not just in new adventures, challenges or dreams – but in people. Find yourself in the arms of those who will fill your tired bones with strength. In people who will bathe you with love and friendship, and never ask for an ounce of it in return. In people who will wrap you with the string of compassion and slip their hearts between the cracks inside yours – showing you that they're no different to you and you're no different to them. Find yourself in gracious smiles and chuckles that crackle through the rainy air.

Find yourself in people whose love is so contagious that it flurries through the small space between you both and uncovers your heart between your weathered ribs. Find yourself in the corners of their fingertips that brush against yours during discomfort, and in their eyes, which gleam with ease. Don't just find yourself in your own journey but in the journey of those that care. The people who are meant for you will make your life better in every single way.

The people who love you will always have a reason to stay.

Healing is always easier when others are by your side. And when you start believing this, your path to heal will turn into an adventurous, worthwhile ride.

Love Yourself

What does it mean to love yourself?

Let me tell you what it doesn't mean. It doesn't mean being selfish. It doesn't mean being aggressive or egotistical. It doesn't mean prioritising your needs over other people's, time and time again. It doesn't mean spending all your money on clothes and gadgets, unless they make you happy – but remember, you will never find true happiness in contingent objects. You will always want the next gadget, the next item of clothing, the next *'high'* until you admit that the love that you give yourself must come from deep within.

Loving yourself doesn't mean expending all your energy in pampering others either. It doesn't mean doing everything for others and nothing for yourself. It doesn't mean giving yourself the bare minimum while offering others everything that you've got. It doesn't mean saying *'okay'* to their half-hearted attempts just because you don't want to upset them.

Loving yourself means saying *'yes'* to selfcare, to putting yourself first – but not at the expense of others. Loving yourself means pampering yourself and taking extra care when listening to your heart. It means trying to figure out what you need. It means making a list of goals and dreams that will furnish your life and aiming to paint your life with contentment. Loving yourself means understanding yourself better.

Loving yourself doesn't mean troubling others for your own

joy. It means taking into consideration what other people need but also focusing on what's meant for you.

Loving yourself is a balance of caring about your wellbeing, but also considering other people's welfare and abiding by your responsibility towards them.

Imperfection

It's easy to drown in self-doubt. It's easy to look at your face in the mirror with the voice at the back of your head telling you that you don't have the potential to be someone, or to make a change – no matter how big or small – in the lives of others. Because giving up is more straightforward and clear-cut, but the route to a meaningful life is often tangled up in difficulties and struggles, in insecurities and questions, such as;

What if I don't make it? What if I fail in this?

This is what we need to fix. It's easy to see failure as something that tarnishes your timeline or makes you seem *less* than others. It's harder to see failure as an example, as a red flag that had to flash before your eyes for you to step away from that path and head towards what's right for you. It's hard to look at situations that haven't worked out in your life as blessings in disguise, rather than as a result of your own flawed actions – ones that can't contribute to your development.

But listen, you tried, and it didn't work out. Whether it was a job, relationship or new project, the point is – you tried. You did your very best. That's what truly matters. That's what defines this failure – and all those before it – as meaningful. As essential for this course in life that you need to take.

I need you to absorb the truth, no matter how bitter, that you will make mistakes. You will fall and stay there for a while. You will give up on people that once gave you life. You will have regrets that pile up high in the compartment of stuff that you don't like remembering, shoved in a corner of your mind. You will want to change the past and wish for a better future while forgetting the present for a while.

But life doesn't stop. You keep living and you keep growing. That is what's important. That is what matters more than anything. That's what will push you forward into new adventures. These adventures will in turn bring with them more losses and gains, as well as mistakes and regrets. But you will have a lifetime of memories as a result.

You need to understand that you're human and bound to fail sometimes.

All you can do is learn from those failures and acknowledge that even after you tried your best, sometimes life isn't in your control – and it's okay. As long as you realise that you will be fine. As long as you know what you need to do, and even if you don't – as long as you're confident that one day, you will figure it out.

Slowly. Steadily.

But you will.

Put Yourself First

Putting yourself first isn't being selfish. Saying no to spending time with others so you can dedicate those extra hours towards your goals isn't being selfish. Taking time away from the chaos of everyday life to stay indoors isn't being selfish. It's called being at one with yourself. It's called working hard to achieve your dreams. It's called finally taking care of your heart, which you've let get throttled over every time you put others needs before you. And now you've finally grasped that you need to do what's necessary to promote your own wellbeing, and you've identified that your dreams won't achieve themselves – because they require you to put in the time and effort into them.

Don't let someone tell you that you're selfish when you *say no*. Don't let someone tell you that you're selfish when you would rather be alone or working hard towards your goals. Don't let someone tell you that you're selfish when you want to keep away from everyone for a while because you need peace and quiet. They can't accept that you've changed for the better, or how much you're willing to do for yourself. And that's fine – because their perspective is different to yours. But if you aren't telling them how to live their life then they shouldn't be telling you how to live yours. Remember this; Putting yourself first and focusing on your wellbeing isn't being selfish. It's called being generous to your heart and caring to your soul. It's called being attentive to your mind. It's called being the only way that you should be if you want to rely on yourself for the abundant life that you seek.

Striking the balance between loving yourself and loving others.

One of the biggest obstacles in my life – when I was considering what it means to love myself – was being able to answer the two questions below:

1. At what point do I stop putting myself first and appreciate that someone else's wellbeing matters more than my own?

2. Where do I cross the line between the two points below?
   a. Other people's perception of me does not define me.
   b. I should take other people's honest views into consideration if I am to allow myself to grow?

The questions are straightforward. They appeal to our basic intuitions about what it means to love yourself and others, and what it means to be sure of yourself, while remaining self-critical so you can reach optimal growth as a person.

There are five beliefs at stake here:

i. Drawing the line between self-love and selfishness.

Drawing the line between self-rejection and selflessness.

ii. Appreciating the truth that someone else's negative perception of you doesn't define you.

Appreciating the truth that other people's brutally honest views are often vital for self-reflection to take place.

* * * *

Drawing the line between self-love and selfishness.
Drawing the line between self-rejection and selflessness.

Let's go over the first question. I will summarise the question: *"When is it okay to put yourself first?"*

I'm not entirely sure of what's right or wrong in a regimented sense, but I've managed to figure out some stuff. The first being this; you shouldn't put people before you to such an extent that it negatively influences your mental, emotional or physical health. If you're denying yourself love and care because you're constantly putting others first, then you're acting in opposition to what self-love requires of you.

Self-love demands us to take into consideration our *needs, emotions* and *health*. This means saying *'no'* when someone asks you to do something for them if it's at odds with those three. Self-love asks you to be there for yourself so you can be there for others. That means putting your welfare first, taking care of yourself and not carrying out actions that will contradict with your mental/emotional health. That's why we shouldn't put other people's needs before our own to such an extent that it contravenes with the love, care and respect that we're required to pour into ourselves.

On the other hand, if you keep putting yourself first without taking into consideration the adverse effect that it will have on those around you – then you're acting selfishly.

"When isn't it okay to put yourself first?"

First, let's understand our responsibility towards others.

When you care about someone and engage in a relationship with them – whether it's romantic, a friendship or familial – you have responsibility to be there for them and to take care of them as much as your physical and mental capacities allow you to. When you deny those who care about you, the relevant love and care that they're entitled to – you're acting in opposition to selflessness. In order to embrace your humanity, you need to learn to put others first on many occasions, even when it's at odds with *what you want* sometimes.

Remember, *what you want* is different to *what you need and deserve*. If putting others before you, contravenes with what you need and deserve, then you should stop. However, if putting others before you is at odds with your own *desires*, then you have a responsibility towards them and regardless of what you want – you should go ahead with doing what's right for them. For example, your friend asks you to go to a restaurant – somewhere that they've always wanted to go and can't imagine sharing that experience with anyone but you – and you say yes. If, on that day, you were to fall terribly ill and needed rest, then self-love requires you to tell your friend that you're not feeling okay, so you would like to reschedule.

This falls in line with both self-love and the responsibility of care that you have towards them.

However, if the restaurant date with your friend arrives and you suddenly want to go to a café with another friend because you're craving pancakes – you have a duty of care *towards your first friend*. On this occasion it would be selfish to cancel on them for your desire to have pancakes with someone else. By denying those who care about you, and whom you have a responsibility towards, the love and care that they're entitled to, you're acting in opposition to selflessness. In order to embrace your humanity, you need to operate with a certain level of selflessness.

For this reason, you need to strike a balance between putting others' needs first, as well as ensuring that you prioritise your own mental and emotional health. This will allow you to enjoy the presence of those around you, along with appreciating your own wellbeing. A by-product of enjoying other people's presence means that a huge amount of that love and care for you will come from them too – this is one of the benefits of pouring your time and energy into those that love you.

But it's not easy and we're completely fallible. And sometimes you will make mistakes. But as long as you let good intentions guide you and act in a way *that aims to* benefit the lives of those that you care about, as well as benefit your own – you will naturally experience an abundance in your relationships and your overall wellbeing.

* * * *

Appreciating the truth that someone else's negative perception of you doesn't define you.

Appreciating the truth that other people's brutally honest views about us are vital for self-reflection to take place.

As a young girl, I always let other people's judgements guide me. If someone complimented my hair, I would do the same hairstyle for days after that. If they didn't like my clothes, I would give my style up completely. If they told me that they liked my personality, then I'd try my best to remember exactly how I behaved with them and replicate it with others. Basically, I would hold on to the good/bad words people said to me and apply it to my behaviour. I would live up to their expectations of me.

But this was self-destructive. I was living according to other people's opinions rather than building a fierce, definitive character for myself, one that couldn't be moulded (well, partly – as there is essential growth that's an inevitable consequence of the years passing.)

As I grew up, I stopped listening to other people altogether. Instead, I focused on the person that *I wanted to be*. This worked out great for me. I boasted confidence. I was sociable. I made great friends and networked with innumerable people who appreciated my worldview and bold personality.

But this eventually backfired too. I started taking criticism lightly. I wouldn't listen to my well-wishers when they recommended something that would benefit me. I wouldn't take into consideration their suggestions for how best to achieve my goals and dreams. I thought that I had it all figured out by myself, so I didn't need to listen to other people's opinions. I became self-reliant in the *hard sense*. I wouldn't pay attention to any external ideas, opinions or suggestions – regardless of whether they were good or bad.

Refusing to listen to other people's advice – as a response to letting them define me while growing up – was counterintuitive.

Being confident is great. It means that you have faith in yourself and can problem-solve. But listening to those who are close to you and want the best for you can open your perspective. Even if you don't agree with them – it may widen your vision to something that you didn't consider if you hadn't heard them out.

So, this is the dilemma – when do we welcome another's honesty and when do we not?

Because we must love ourselves too, and self-love requires removing negative opinions that could tarnish your self-esteem and people who can dim your light. The way I see it is this: *focus on intention*. It's important to be self-reflective. And sometimes this involves taking into consideration other people's ideas – this could be about you, your work or your behaviour. And the only time that you should do this is when they say it with *good intent* – with a heart that only wants the best for you.

There may be some people in your life who will try their best to bring you down. People who will never stop to give you a helping hand. People who will never truly be happy in your success. It's their views that you should brush away and not take seriously. Their opinions don't matter, nor do they define who you are as a person. On the other hand – there are people who care about you from the core. People who only want to see you blossom. People who want your happiness and can't wait for you to become the best version of yourself. People who will do everything in their power to urge you on. People who will always cheer for you from the side-line and be genuinely pleased for your every success. It's their views that you should listen to. Their opinions are the ones that that you should take into consideration, note down and include in your mental list of revisions on how to better your life

Because what they think of you matters.

The rest of them – those who don't care, who don't want you to do well, who don't think twice before they say something hurtful or for whom your feelings don't matter – their views don't matter.

Only listen to those who care about you and remember – you don't have to take their opinions seriously if you don't want to. But take their views on board anyway. Because being self-critical doesn't mean taking *every single person's* opinion seriously – especially those with hostile ones. It doesn't mean letting people purposely bring you down or be rude to you. It doesn't mean giving others the opportunity to question your dreams and hopes or dim your light.

Being self-critical means assessing your shortcomings with the aim to improve. It means valuing the suggestions of those who care about you and want the best for you. It means drinking up the honest opinions of others when they come from a place of good intent – no matter how bitter it is. Lastly, being self-critical means opening your eyes and mind on how to nurture your soul and become the best version of yourself – which includes acknowledging the honest views of those who want the best for you.

Apologise

I'm sorry to those whom I hurt while I was hurting. I didn't mean the hurtful stuff that I said. I wish that I could change the past. I wish that I was softer with your heart. But I can't change what happened and – unfortunately – my actions may have cracked through your heart and I can only apologise for it.

The one thing that hurting on the hands of others has allowed me to see is that, sometimes, I will be the one who causes the damage. I will be the reason for spilled tears and wet cheeks, the person behind all the heartache that carried on for weeks and could've been avoided if I had taken more care. If I had been more sensitive. If I had been kinder or softer to your heart. And it fills me with guilt when I remember the number of occasions that I've injured other people's souls in the process of fixing my own.

But all I can do now is apologise. I hope that your heart doesn't ache as much as it did then. I hope that one day you can find it within you to forgive me. For not saying the right words. For not letting you down gently. For being a horrible friend. For not being there for you when I should have been.

I was just trying to find my way.

But I'm so sorry that you lost yours in the process.

Growth

Sometimes, I'm unable to grasp the magnitude of my growth. Not the, *'I'm a much better person now'*, but the, *'Even if I'm still flawed, I am enlightened in my journey of it all'*.

I often forget that having a heart with torn edges says a lot more about you than a heart that is gleaming red and unscathed by the bleak reality of life that affects many of us. Going through hardships and getting scarred in the process doesn't make you any less beautiful. Trust me. But sometimes I don't see it in this way. I think that all my experiences have tarnished me and darkened my aura to the point where I don't have anything left to offer. Where, if others were to spend time with me – all they would get is dirt on their soul. Of course, I've understood now that thinking about myself in this way is wrong. Believing this about myself is toxic and self-destructive.

We need to accept that our wounds don't make us any less deserving of love or light. But that's our problem. We fail to admit how far we've come because the past trauma or loss still follow us like a dark shadow on the brightest day of the year, forcing us to forget all the reasons we have to be happy. Forcing us to forget how grateful we are for the life that we've been given.

Healing is hard.

Heck, it's the hardest journey that we take. It demands so much out of us. And no one could understand this better than

I do. But you need to welcome the truth that the light exists. Even if it arrives a little late and not when you want it to. Even if it's uncomfortable when you first face it. Even if it hurts more and heals less in the beginning. It arrives. It arrives when it's supposed to. It arrives when you least expect it. It arrives when you need it the most.

It arrives when the time is right – because that's when you should grab onto it and never let it go.

Dear Self

I hurt someone badly. Should I stop loving myself?

The answer to this is simple: **no.** You shouldn't stop loving yourself because you hurt someone else. Especially if your heart was in the right place, if your intentions were good and if you didn't want to cause them pain but – because of the circumstances – had to.

One of the most important lessons that we learn when it comes to self-love is this – *we are imperfect*. We're fallible. Emotional. We're going to make mistakes, upset others and play a part in their growth. We're going to be the lessons that people receive and the regrets that they wish they could change – which is okay. Wounding others and making mistakes doesn't strip away your value as a person.

No one is intentionally evil or harsh. Okay, *maybe some people are*. People who find joy in hurting others and acting in a way that unsettles their lives. But this isn't reflective of most of us. Those rare, toxic humans don't represent us all. Sure, some people can be intentionally evil – but the rest of us aren't like that. We don't wake up in the morning and ask ourselves the question, *'Who am I going to hurt today?'*, because it's not the way we work. We don't receive pleasure from causing others pain. It's for this reason that when it does happen, and we're the reason behind other people's misery – it makes us feel terribly guilty.

People getting hurt is a result in at least one of the following:

i.   When you speak the bitter truth which, in a lot of cases, is painful to hear.

ii.   When they don't get what they want.

iii.   When reality doesn't coincide with their expectations – these usually involve you and your treatment of them.

iv.   When, on the rare occasion, you lose your cool and shout at them/ treat them poorly.

v.   When you let them down.

Let me point out that stuff happens. Things go wrong. It's an essential part of life.

You can't please everyone – especially with the knowledge that neither you nor they are perfect.

You're constantly adapting, making mistakes and dealing with your own issues. Your paths cross with others for a reason. Sometimes they hurt you in order for you to gain invaluable insight and sometimes you're the one that needs to hurt them. Sometimes you need to show them what they're doing wrong

– even if it's through causing them discomfort or breaking their heart.

The following two truths go hand in hand:

1. You are an individual who is deserving of love, care and respect.
2. You may hurt people, break their heart or do something they don't like that will form an invaluable learning curve for them.

I'm not saying that it's okay to be rude, mean or heartless. It's not okay to disrespect people, be ruthless or carry out actions that cause them emotional suffering and still say; *'I am worthy of all the love that I give to myself'*. You can't be malicious then use, *'I'm human and imperfect'*, as a justification. I'm not saying that every time we injure other people's hearts, we're excused for it because we taught them something.

We are – in every way – *guilty*.

But what I am saying is this; your mistakes don't define you.

Yes, you did something wrong. You made someone feel bad. You might regret what you did and wish to go back and fix it. But all you can do now is learn from it and move on. Your heart may have been in the right place, but your actions didn't benefit them – at least not in the short-term. Rather than getting upset over this truth – *you need to let go of it*. Tell yourself that you will do better. That you will be kinder. Gentler. Softer. Tell yourself that if you come across a predicament of this sort again, you will try your hardest to let the situation disperse gently.

Making mistakes is a part of being human. But making mistakes doesn't turn us into a bad person.

Without getting too philosophical about good/bad actions, this is how I make a distinction between a *'good mistake'* and a *'bad mistake'*:

a. The intention with which you make that mistake.
b. The resulting reflection – the urge (or lack, thereof) to learn from the mistake and the goal of becoming a better person.
c. The desire to give an apology.
d. The change in future interactions of the same sort.

Your moral theory will also determine the level of guilt that you attach to the action that you carried out. For instance, if you see actions as *intrinsically good/bad* then you won't agree with the points above because – for you – *the act of hurting someone is wrong*.

I use an *'intention-consequences'* approach when assessing actions/people who carry those actions out as *'good'* or *'bad'* and, according to this, if your intentions were good then you are not a bad person, even if the actions caused them discomfort. But this isn't set in stone and it doesn't mean that actions can't be bad even if the intention was good. It all depends on your intuition and how you approach the situation. I would never say that breaking someone's heart is a good action in itself.

But what I do say is this – if you had to do it to save them from further agony, then *you are not a bad person*. If the action brought them happiness in the long term, then *it is not a bad action.*

The same applies to the other 3 points – guilt can transform a person for the better. The desire for an apology and the need to *'reform'* will add weight to whether your action was right/wrong. Lastly, the way that you model your future interactions of the same sort will also determine whether your intentions were to hurt the other person or whether the original action was indeed out of your control.

Without going in too much detail on moral rightness/wrongness – otherwise this chapter will turn into a Philosophy essay and I haven't written one of those in years – the basic idea that you should take from this is that *you are not a bad person.* Especially when it wasn't your intention to hurt the other person. Especially if you tried your best to do everything right but it turned wrong anyway.

You are just human.

You're not a horrible person because you hurt someone. So, stop worrying about what you said and what you did. What is done is done. If you haven't apologised already – drop them a message, call them, organise a meeting and get it off your chest. Apologise to them to let go of the guilt that you're carrying on your shoulders. Then move on from this.

Don't let your mistakes weaken the hold on your self-worth.

Remember this: you are still deserving of love, care and respect and hurting others doesn't make you a horrible person.

Saying 'No'

As part of being good people, we feel bad when we don't do something for others. We give explanations for why we cancelled on dinner and we justify our sadness on a day when everyone is supposed to be happy. We assume that it's okay to meet up with an old friend or give emotional support to a previous lover because *they need us* and – as a result of the history that we shared – we have an obligation to be there for them. But by doing this we're being unfair on ourselves.

You don't owe anyone anything.

You don't owe people an explanation for your actions. Because those who love you will understand why you didn't turn up to dinner, why you were sad or why you need time away from them. Just because you're a good person it doesn't mean that you should go above and beyond for everyone – especially when you're struggling with your own mental/emotional health. If you're going through a difficult time in your life, then it's okay to *say no*. It's okay to inform them that you want to spend some time alone and you don't want to go out – even if it's out of character. Even if it's to the people who always look out for you. Even if it's to your partner, to your family or your friends.

If you need time – *you take it*. You shouldn't feel guilty about it – because putting yourself first isn't a crime. Taking care of yourself before you can take care of others is a priority.

You don't owe people anything. You do things for people

because you love and care for them. Because life is happier with them around. Because they've always looked out for you and you appreciate that. Because they're your best friends, your family, and you want to be there for them.

You don't throw a surprise party for your best friend because you owe it to them. You don't put your work aside and give time to your close ones because you owe it to them. You don't offer your shoulder to your loved ones to cry on because you owe it to them. You don't make plans to go out, go on holidays or show concern to others because you owe it to them. *You do it because you care.* You do it because they deserve it. Because you want them to be happy. Because you love them. Because you *want to* and not because you *have to*. And you don't owe old friends who left you at the worst time in your life, or previous lovers because of whom you were in that horrible state to begin with, your time or your attention.

You don't owe anyone anything besides yourself.

The day you admit this to yourself, you will stop telling yourself that you're not enough for people. It will be the day you start putting yourself first without feeling guilty about it. It will be the day that you will appreciate that all the effort you put into others comes from your *love* and not your *duty*.

Dear Self

The time I broke the heart of someone I deeply cared about.

I love having genuine friendships with people – regardless of whether they're male or female. I never understood the stereotypical phrase, *'A guy and girl can never be just friends'*, and throughout my school years, I got on really well with my guy friends – sometimes even more than the female ones. It's not that I had a problem with any of the girls in my year. They were just as lovely as the guys, but I just had a better time with my guy friends.

We exchanged careless banter and laughed, and I found it easier to express my views about stuff without the fear that they would judge me. They were also excellent advice givers. It's for this reason that, growing up, I enjoyed the company of my guy friends quite a lot.

But when I look back, I recall that several of those friendships ended in tears or a broken heart – most of the time theirs, and sometimes my own.

Let me clarify that I'm not speaking in binaries. I'm not saying that a guy and girl can never be *just friends*, but what I am saying is this – most of *my friendships* with men have ended horribly because of romantic feelings. Blergh. In fact, the first person who broke my heart – and because of whom I started writing about moving on – was in fact *my friend of 8 years*. We'd never dated or gotten into a relationship.

You ask me – what does this have to do with self-worth?

It is simple, isn't it? No? *Okay, fine.* Let me explain it in detail.

In basic terms – a lot of the time those friendships ended because I said '*no*'. The feelings weren't mutual. I didn't like them back and as a result our friendship ended. In short – I caused them distress. Lots of it. *It was me. All me.* On a few occasions, I also got hurt. But I'll go into that in a different chapter.

For now, what I want you to grasp is that *the hurt was caused by me.* I was the culprit.

Usually, when we experience pain because of someone, we start telling ourselves that they truly sucked as a person. At least in the beginning. Perhaps we don't truly have this opinion about them, but these negative thoughts are a good way to take the first step to get over them. We tell ourselves that this person was horrible. They didn't treat us right and – if they wanted to – they could've saved us from the spools of tears that we've shed because of them.

Eventually, when we're out of that bubble of darkness, we acknowledge that it wasn't meant to be, and they did what they had to. Of course, that's not always the case. Sometimes they really are mean people who treated us badly and are warranted the criticism/disliking that we do even after we're over them.

But a lot of the time, this is just a tool that we use to push ourselves as further away from them as we can. Once we're over them we realise that we only badmouthed them to move on and they weren't horrible people. Not completely anyway. But this doesn't occur to us when we're grieving. As the infamous phrase goes – the easiest way to get over someone is to hate them. To start off with anyway. Also, I don't know where I heard that phrase. Maybe I made it up. Anyway, let's 'move on', (*see what I did there, haha*).

Now, the possibility of *us hurting someone* and them having these negative thoughts about us is unfeasible. I can't be one of those heartbreakers who doesn't think twice before she says something, or someone who leads another person on without a care for their emotions. I would never do that to someone. Impossible. *I can't suck.* I'm supposed to be perfect(!)

The truth is that we do injure other people's hearts – causing them the kind of discomfort that isn't necessary and can be avoided if we put some thought into our actions and calculated the consequences. We're human and fallible and, unfortunately, we will say and do things that other people don't like. We will act in a way that doesn't fall in accordance with their expectations and what they're owed and, often, we won't realise it.

I'm aware that this is difficult for you – someone who tries their best to be good – to come to terms with. You know what it's like to get hurt. You know how much it kills when you like someone, and they don't return your feelings. You've been led on in the past. You're certain that you wouldn't do the same to others. You couldn't.

But as hard as it is to accept – unfortunately, *sometimes you do*.

And I know how it feels. Because I, too, have a harder time being the reason for someone else's pain than I do when they're the reason for mine. When I get hurt, I tell myself that it's okay because the other person played a part in my journey. I reassure myself that there's a better plan in place for me. They weren't the right person, that's all. I will make it through this. I'm certain that I will. I can move on.

My friends also support me by pointing out all the good that will come out of this experience. They point out the lesson, and often they do this by calling out what was wrong with the other person's actions. *'That guy was a loser,'* they say. *'He lost out big time.'*

I know what's going on in your mind.

You're thinking that it's irrational to point out what was wrong with the other person just to make yourself feel better. And I agree. *I do*. But sometimes, hearing those words are essential for you to feel better *in that moment* to give you the courage to move on. As the old expression goes, *'You dodged a bullet'*. Now, even if you didn't physically dodge a bullet, even if they weren't all that bad (I mean, how could they be if you liked them? Unless you're into narcissistic losers like I am), hearing something along the lines of 'You dodged a bullet' is enough to imply that you've been saved. It's enough to make you think that this situation, where you're pining for someone who has troubled your heart, *is in your favour*.

This aching is good for you. In the long run, this pain is better than the one that being with them would've brought you. This hurting is going to aid you. It will build you. You're alive! Yay! You dodged a bullet and you're alive. What could be better than that?

When you're finally out of those simmering weeks or months of agony, you come to terms with the reality that perhaps the other person wasn't all that bad, and they didn't lose out. And neither did you. Not because you're not great or they're not great but because both of you deserve better. Both of you are meant to be with someone else. On this occasion, at least, neither of you lost out. When you get out of that place of self-pity, you will be able to see it all upon reflection. You will remove the heavy lens of self-pity and develop a clearer vision of what happened, what went wrong and what's ahead of you.

But when you're in the ocean of despair, you don't want to hear anything good about the other person. Someone simply justifying the other person's actions is enough to make you boil with anger. That's why all your close people are there to deliver those words of disapproval regarding the person who injured your heart. And they do this to give you the push that you need to take the first step in moving on.

When I turn the same process back to myself, however, – the

possibility that *I have hurt someone* and now they're sitting there, stewing in their misery, moping and rattling with negative opinions about me in their mind, makes me feel horrible. To add to that, if they're going to their friends for advice (which they certainly are), their friends will also spit out words of condemnation towards me. They will probably tell this person that they're better off with me out of their life and how much *I lost out* by not saying *'yes'*. Their friends will shudder with mean words that paint me as heartless, just so this person can move on. Or maybe *I am heartless* – or was – on this occasion and those judgements of my behaviour are as much *honest* as they are *vital* for them to move on.

But the potential/actuality of this happening is terrible.

I don't want other people to judge me or talk badly about me. I don't want to be the one who disturbs someone else's peace. *I don't want to be heartless.* But when has life ever coincided with what we want?

Let me go into the story.

Earlier I spoke about making a few wonderful friends who made my life so much better. Amongst them was a friend who arrived in my life as a bright, beautiful ray of light. He was funny. Charismatic. Kind-hearted. Weird. Goofy. And an absolute joy to be around. My smile would spread from cheek to cheek and not leave for hours when we were together. There was never a dull moment when he was around. I always looked forward to when I would see him next, and I cherished the time that we spent together.

Him, another girl and I were the best of friends. We were *the three musketeers.* We went everywhere together, divulging in jokes, engaging in crazy antics and falling over with stomach-aching chuckles every time. These two friends surrounded me with a blissful, glimmering bubble of euphoria. Even writing about it now puts a nostalgic smile on my face, because that's how much fun we used to have.

Unfortunately, just like the bad moments in our lives, the good moments don't last forever either.

If our interactions had been based solely on friendship, then perhaps he would've still been in my life. But they weren't. And as time went on, he started developing feelings for me which I couldn't reciprocate. Initially I found him cute, in a boyish way. His innocence was admirable and when I first saw him, I had a slight crush on him. But that's the thing with crushes – they disappear in a blink.

The more that I got to know him the more I understood that I only found him endearing and adorable – like a younger brother. But I didn't like him romantically. I enjoyed spending time with him, but I couldn't imagine being in a relationship with him.

Because the truth is that I was looking for something – more specifically, *someone* – else.

This friend was genuinely wonderful. It was a shame because if I had said yes, he would've tried his best to make me very happy. But I wouldn't have been in love with him – and I couldn't sacrifice something this significant. Maybe if it had been 5 years from then – where I was 27 and he was 25 – and I hadn't found 'the one', I might have said yes. I don't know what future Ruby was going to react to that kind of situation. Ruby at 22 was completely against *settling*. Having said that, I'm Ruby at 25 and I'm still against it. I guess I haven't changed after all.

The age gap was a small factor that contributed to my 'no'. Because I could tell from the interactions that we had that he needed to do some growing up. The second reason for my 'no' was the lack of spark between us. And there was one final factor to take into consideration – I liked someone else, but I'll go into this one some other time. Trust me, it's a story that you don't want to miss.

I know what a lot of you are thinking – *what's the big deal?*

He liked you. You didn't like him back. He should've appreciated your honesty and agreed to continue being your friend. This is how the situation should pan out, right? It's okay to have a friend who likes you, but you don't like back. It's inconvenient but it's okay. It's not the end of the world.

Especially if you tackle it early on and make it clear from the beginning that nothing can happen, *ever*, and you can only be friends. Nothing more. Those creases in your friendship can be ironed out if you sit down and communicate the concerns as soon as they arise. Over here, they can identify their position and you can identify yours by telling them that you don't feel the same way. And, if they value your friendship more than their desire to be with you and are happy to be in your life as a friend, then you both can continue your friendship exactly as it is.

I thought that this is what we'd done.

When we sat down in Starbucks, our hands wrapped around paper cups letting off the steam of fresh coffee, eyelashes fluttering plentifully as we tossed explanations back and forth like netball – I assumed that it was all out on the table. His dark eyes glittered, and a shade of disappointment settled on his golden face as he gulped down what I said. The topic ended there. A decision had been made. It was never going to work.

But I didn't realise how wrong I was.

Looking back, I realise that I hadn't been firm enough with him. I skirted around the truth. When he asked me whether I liked him – his tone silken and kind. His brow furrowed. A stiff, scared look on his gentle face – I didn't give him what he needed to hear in order to move on. My words were thin on honesty, resting on the fringes of the truth. My mouth wobbled with the effort of saying, *'no'*. So, I hurled out a long explanation of why it wouldn't work out instead, hoping that he would register what I meant. Praying that he understood my predicament – that I couldn't give him a hard *'no'* because I didn't want to hurt him.

I didn't want to be the first crack that went through his foetal heart.

It was on this day that everything started to go wrong. His face turned from concern, to confusion, to a mask of expectancy. His responses tingled with conviction, as though my answer hadn't closed all possible doors – which is what I'd wanted to do. I intended to spill the whole truth – the one where him and I working out would never be an option, but I wanted to do it without upsetting him.

That was my biggest mistake. My mistake was *not looking him in the eye* and saying, *'It will **never** happen. If you want me in your life, you can only have me as a friend.'* Instead, every time he mentioned *'If it's meant to be, it will be'*, I would shift uncomfortably in my seat and flutter out a few lines about how much I liked this other guy that I was speaking to. I would purposely expand my eyes with a flare of feelings for this other person – hoping that my expression was as obvious as a *'no'*. This probably did more to steer my friend towards having faith that it might work because he thought that I was trying to make him jealous – to which I can only say: *darn you, millennials!*

Why must our generation play these petty games?

Clearly, there was a reason why he had the false belief that I would lie to make him jealous – because our generation is one where honesty is rarely valued. But I've always been a straightforward person and that's why when I mentioned this other guy that I had feelings for, *I meant it.* It was no game. But my friend didn't take me seriously. At least not until 2 years later when he kicked me out of his life for good. But I will go into that later.

Anyway, let's get back to my story.

What I really wanted to say was, *'No, it won't work out between us'*, without uttering those exact words. I assumed that he received the implicit message loud and clear through my constant mention of someone else and the lack of urging the *'If it's meant to be, it will be'* phrase. But he didn't. Or he did but his vision was coated with blind optimism. He was convinced that it might work, and it won't make sense to you or me because we aren't in his shoes. But we've all been there at some point.

Love works on conviction and leaving it in God/destiny's hands, and ardently following the expression, *'If it's meant to be, it will be.'*

It turns out that my vision was also coated with a resounding surety that prevented me from seeing the truth. I convinced myself that every time this conversation sprung up and my face turned crimson with embarrassment, he understood my true emotions. Or the lack of them. Instead, all he understood was that if he ripped open his heart and showed me how much he could love me – then I would love him too. He tried his very best. He listened to me ramble on about hurting for someone else when his own heart was pining for me. He made me laugh. He was patient when I cried and was there was for me when I needed a friend. He believed that he could change my mind by showing me how well he could treat me.

Perhaps he felt that he was up against the other guy. That somehow, they were both competing for me and if he cared for me more than my other friend then I would choose him instead. His heart raced with certainty that, one day, I would love him back. But I never did.

Two years after it began, our friendship ended devastatingly.

He didn't want anything to do with me because of how much I'd hurt him – but this had never been my intention. I didn't mean to lead him on. I thought that my rejection of his love was as evident as colour of the sky, heck, I told him often about how it wasn't possible. I looked at him with certainty whenever I uttered those words. And every time I mentioned the person *that I did like*, I smiled with surety. I treated it as a normal conversation that we could have together – even though his unrequited feelings for me were the elephant in the room.

I felt absolutely horrible about it later.

As much as I would like to tell myself that I had been obvious in saying, *'no'* – I should have been clearer. When I looked back, speckles of interactions appeared before my eyes; moments when I had the opportunity to tell him clearly that it was never going to work out, kind gestures that sprung from his deep emotions but I waved off as nothing other than one friend helping out another friend, and expressions of true feelings masked in the form of – what I told myself was – harmless flirting and banter.

The weeks that followed the end of our friendship – I drowned in guilt and low self-esteem.

During that period, I lost another friend too – this was the other guy – the one that I liked. At the time I found myself pitted against a storm of dark emotions. I hated myself for hurting my friend. Each night I would go to sleep with a swarm of thoughts buzzing like loud bees in my mind, reminding me that I had royally screwed up this time. This brought back memories of all those occasions in the past when I'd disappointed others because of my inability to say *'no'*. It also triggered recollections of when *I had been harsh,* and it hadn't resulted the way that I'd envisioned.

Many years prior to the incident above, I was 16 and in Sixth

Form and I had a friend who really liked me – but it would have never worked. As someone who was aware of her inability to be strict with her rejections, on that occasion – *I was brutal*. Near the end of our friendship I treated this friend very poorly. I had a justifiable reason for this; if he couldn't move on from me *'normally'* then he had to move on in a different way. I wanted him to hate me so much that he moved on for good. And he did. He hated me to such an extent that when he moved on with his life – he never looked back.

This chapter in my life caused me undeniable distress. I was sopping with guilt over my actions. I couldn't come to terms with the truth that I had the capability to be this mean to someone who cared so much about me. Someone whom I called one of my closest friends. Losing him was hard, especially when his departure left a pedestal that all future guys would be matched against. But, once more – I didn't love him. He was just a friend, albeit a great one whom any girl would be truly lucky to have, but still just a friend.

That's why I had to say *'no'*. That's why I had to be harsh, because he couldn't comprehend my rejection in any other way. That's why I had to sacrifice our friendship – because I wanted him to have a chance at true love later in his life. Perhaps in my harshness and the unfair way that I treated him – I may have broken a huge part of his heart.

It was after this experience that I decided that if anyone else liked me and I didn't like them back – *I would let them down slowly*. Softly. Gently. Nicely. I'd do it however I could, but I would never act in the same way again. But once more, years down the line when I met the friend that I'm telling you all about now, and I refused to be brutal – it still bit me in the ass. If there's one lesson that I've taken from all of these interactions, it is this; regardless of whether you do it the *'right way'* or the *'wrong way',* when you don't reciprocate someone's feelings for you – they will leave you and probably dislike you anyway, at least to begin with.

And I guess they're right in their place to.

They need to prioritise their wellbeing and put themselves first, and if your presence is acting in opposition to that, then they're not wrong to bid you farewell. But this doesn't change how their departure makes you feel: guilt-ridden. Horrible. Mean. Heartless. It causes a hurricane of invalidating opinions of yourself inside you. You start to dislike yourself because you broke someone's heart. You could have saved them from the distress if you really tried.

But you did try. You tried your hardest.

You reflected from your previous experiences and gave it your best shot. You didn't want to repeat your past mistakes. You wanted to do it differently this time. And you did. But you still failed – and it's okay. I know that when you lose people in this way, it jarrs your self-worth. You start to believe that you're a useless, selfish person who's unable to keep other people happy. You tell yourself that you don't deserve love from others if all you're going to do is hurt them. And this is how I felt about myself for the first 2-3 months after I broke my friend's heart. It wasn't the first time and I was sure that it wouldn't be the last, (although, *thank god that it was* – more on that in my next book).

There I was, preaching about self-discovery and being a good person while carrying out actions that made important people in my life hate me and turn away from me.

What was wrong with me?

I continued to simmer in sadness for weeks.

Then one morning, as the sun fractured through the grey clouds towards a clearer sky – it also cleared up my foggy mind.

I'd finally grasped the truth. There is nothing wrong with me or anyone else who hurts someone. Especially if you tried your best to do it right. It's not the end of the world if you cause someone pain or break their heart. It may be the end of the world that they'd envisioned with you – but this was an essential hurdle that they needed to cross in their life in order to see their life clearly again.

Ask yourself this – how many times have other people upset you? Several, right?

Perhaps they came back after a few weeks/months to apologise, but you weren't having any of it. Or, maybe you're a generous person and, overwhelmed with mercy for those who've harmed you, you instantly chose to forgive them. But that's not the point. The point is – you've also been hurt on the hands of others. Sometimes you forgive them. Sometimes you don't. Sometimes you hate them because that hatred acts as a catalyst for you to move on in your life before it hits you like a brick – weeks or months down the line – that this person didn't mean to crack your heart open. It had to happen.

If you're a reflective person then you're able to see a message in every wound that was caused by others. These wounds were vital for you to become an elevated version of yourself. Maybe you're even thankful to them for the pain that they caused you. *I know that I am.*

Even though I've witnessed some of the darkest moments of my life on the hands of others – I'm grateful for every second of the darkness that I faced. I'm not a sadist. I promise. I'm merely a reflective human. I wouldn't be who I am without the hard lessons that those people taught me. A few of them wounded me intentionally and – whether my perception of them changed or not – their perception of themselves *would never change.* They still saw themselves as worthy, loveable individuals – despite treating me poorly.

In that case, why should my perception of myself change? Why did I feel undeserving after letting my friend down, or conclude that no one should be my friend or love me because of it? Why couldn't I grasp the insight from it, like I did whenever *other people let me down?*

Over time, *I have learned to.*

I've figured out that my self-worth isn't dependent on the mistakes that I make, especially when the intention behind those mistakes was one of compassion. I don't mean to torment others. In fact, I try to do the total opposite. I aim to act in a way that will minimise the pain for them, but sometimes it doesn't work out. For instance, in the case of my friend, I tried my best and the results weren't what I expected. That is fine. It's okay. It means that I need to try harder next time. Or do something different. Or reflect on what the situation demands of me. And if I get it wrong on that occasion too – then I need to try harder again. Or I could accept that breaking other people's heart *will never be easy*. It will never come without guilt. But I can't let this get to me or allow it to determine the love that I have for myself.

I'm not a bad person. I know that I'm not.

And over time, I've accepted that this had to happen. I was a key tool in the lesson they inevitably had to learn. A lesson that taught them not to glue their happiness to someone else. A lesson that told them to accept that their value didn't reside in chasing someone who didn't love them back. A lesson that reflected the harsh reality that sometimes *what you want is not what you need*. I have learnt through others, and others have to learn through me. Of course, this realisation doesn't strip off the guilt or suddenly make me happy when I injure other people's hearts. It doesn't take the weight off my shoulders when my actions have made them miserable.

But it does mean that *I no longer hate myself for it*. I no longer reprimand myself for my mistakes. Instead, I dive into what I can learn as well and how, if at all, I can act differently next time.

That's what I want you all to take from this.

Read my words clearly: it's inevitable that you will break hearts and create a storm in other people's lives.

You need to welcome this as a part of you as all the other things that you're proud of are. Hurting other people doesn't lower your value as a person. It doesn't turn you evil. It doesn't say anything bad about you. It doesn't define you. Hurting other people is part of being human. It's a consequence of being imperfect. It comes with being flawed. It proves that *you are not* all-knowing, all-loving or all-powerful like God/a higher reality/a powerful entity.

You're only human. So, learn from your mistakes and *move on*.

Read this clearly – you're not unworthy because you caused someone pain. Instead, what you did promotes their growth as well as yours. It helps you both. It forms a chapter in both your lives – albeit under different titles of *'regrets'* and *'lessons'* – which contributes to the big book called *'life'*. I hope that you can let this truth settle in every curve of your heart and not hate yourself whenever you make someone upset. Remember, you're not at fault.

Please – let it go and move forward in your life.

There is so much still left in this world for you to experience. Don't let your mistakes stop you from enjoying your qualities. Just let it go and be happy.

They will receive their share of happiness one day and so will you.

Be Brave

Be brave enough to be alone.

By alone, I mean not relying on someone else for your happiness or your comfort. By alone I mean dreaming of a future where your goals depend on you – and only you – to achieve them. By alone I mean strolling down a beach with the sand between your feet and hugging yourself as the wind ripples against your arms. By alone I mean taking yourself on a date to your favourite café with a book and a coffee, watching the sun rise and fall, and feeling only comfort in that moment.

Be brave enough to love yourself. By love I mean wrapping strength around your wrists as you bunch your hands into tight fists for anyone who dares to treat you badly, and letting your heart rest inside your chest rather than carrying it on your sleeve for people who will never see it for what it's worth. Love yourself enough to walk away, enough to say 'no' when you've had enough, enough to smile at your reflection in the mirror when life is grim, enough to strip away the guilt attached to putting yourself first.

Be brave enough to be there for yourself.

By being there for yourself, I mean holding your own hand when it gets too much, wiping your tears when you're settled in a tight corner of your room with nothing but a human-sized shadow resting beside you. I mean giving yourself the compulsory pep talks, the heart-to-hearts, listening to your worries/concerns and holding your falling pieces together as close as you can. Because if you don't then you will fall apart and there will be no one else there to save you.

Be brave enough to say 'no'. Say no when you have had enough. Say no when you don't want to give yourself away anymore. Say no when you don't want to be pushed around or forced to take part in anything that doesn't fulfil you, and when your heart clatters against your ribs because it's been drained of all the love and affection that it could give.

Be brave enough to become the right person for yourself. Because if you're brave enough to do what is right for your heart, then I promise you – you will never feel lonely when you're alone.

I am Happy

All I ever do these days is smile.

It's as though my lips have permanently planted themselves into an upwards curve, spreading wide across my cheeks and making my eyes squint the way they do whenever I'm happy. *And I am happy.* Happy in every essence, in every sense of the word. But this doesn't mean that some days aren't hard or difficult to live through, or that I never get sad. Because I'm human after all. And to be human means to live through every emotion in its depth, including the negative ones.

But the dark moments don't eat at my peace anymore. In fact, they add to it. When I'm sad I recognise what contributes to making my life valuable. I appreciate it, and when I'm happy again – I truly absorb those moments once more. I welcome light and love into my life once sadness takes its leave.

All I ever do is smile these days.

And, believe me – I'm scared. I'm scared to lose my smile, as well as the reason for it. But I have faith in God and the plan bigger than me that's always guided me towards what was meant for me. It's for this reason that I've finally let happiness in without worrying too much about whether it will stay. That's why I no longer get too upset when it leaves, because I'm certain that sadness will never stay for longer than it's meant to. That's why all I ever do is smile these days – because I wouldn't want to have it any other way.

Dear Self

Self-love and self-worth. What do they mean to me?

Writing about my self-worth hasn't been easy. Neither has loving myself. It's an uphill battle, one that I struggle with daily, as I know that a lot of us do. Some days, I tell myself that I've got it figured out. Some days, I'm sure of my worth and I'm certain that the only thing that I expect from other people is to treat me with actions that live up to this truth – including myself. But other days, it's hard.

You see, when you've lived in a world that has trained you to love yourself in fragments – loving yourself wholly isn't something that you're used to. It's hard to challenge this idea of *fragmented self-love* with the real one. The one that is kinder to our hearts and lighter on our souls. The one that tells us to love ourselves wholly. Entirely. Including every imperfection, insecurity and scar. With all our heart and soul. It's for this reason that I choose to focus most of my writing on self-love and self-worth. Because a lot of us struggle with it. A lot of us find it difficult to push away ideas that we've been handed down in small parcels of self-denial and rejection and welcome ideas about acceptance, growth and fallibility, combined with a high sense of self.

It's for this reason that I write about this stuff. I want to emphasise on the importance of it and push for it during our healing. Because high self-esteem and an abundance of self-love would prevent so many negative experiences in our lives. The world would be gentler if we were gentle with ourselves. The world wouldn't question our imperfections if we wore them like our armour in battlefield. The world would be kinder to us if we were kinder to ourselves.

Because, in the end, it all falls into place once we love and appreciate ourselves.

But what does it mean to love yourself?

What does it mean to have self-worth?

Firstly, let me unpick these two because a lot of the time they're used interchangeably when they don't have the same meaning. Self-love and self-worth are two different words.

Self-love is the act of prioritising your happiness and wellbeing.

When you love yourself, you pay attention to your needs and carry out actions to take care of yourself. When you love yourself, you don't settle for less and, primarily, you acknowledge *what* is less to begin with. This guides you in making the right decisions that promote your wellbeing and serve you.

Self-worth doesn't involve *acting* in the way that self-love does.

Self-worth is a frame of mind towards yourself which contributes to actions that fall under self-love.

Therefore, when you love yourself, you act in a way that results in the overall betterment of your life. One of the contributing factors to loving yourself is having high self-regard – this comes with self-worth. If you have positive self-worth, then you will carry out loving actions and nurture your happiness wholeheartedly.

As you can see, self-worth and self-love are deeply intertwined. Decline in one will result in decline in the other. For instance, if you have low self-worth then you will assume that you don't deserve love or approval from anyone – specifically, from yourself. As a result, this will cause you to neglect what's good for you and refrain from acting to improve your overall wellbeing.

In simple terms, if you develop high self-worth through appreciation, self-reflection and care then you will act in the name of self-love. This means not tolerating other people's flawed definitions of what a *'good'* person looks like. Denying validation of their views of beauty, grace and perfection. Refusing to endorse their perception of you. And being unwelcome to harsh criticism or bad treatment that comes from a place of resentment and, instead, prioritising your own needs. Putting your joy first. Putting your wellbeing first.

This means being there for yourself when you need it the most. Loving yourself, despite your limitations and your blunders. Despite your misgivings, your past or your uncertain future. This means gripping your hand tightly in moments of distress, and most importantly when you might crumble. This means standing tall in the face of darkness and never letting the light within you wither away. It also means taking on board the truth that you're flawed and sometimes you will carry out actions that are wrong — but those actions don't define you. Your soft heart defines you. Your generous behaviour defines you. Your caring nature defines you. You going out of your way to give a helping hand to those that you love defines you. Your intentions define you.

When you develop a positive frame of mind towards yourself, as a result having a determined sense of self-worth, you will treat yourself with love. You will put more effort into understanding yourself and you will value every part of your soul.

That's the true beauty of letting positive self-worth into your life and acting in the name of self-love.

Heartbreak/ Moving On

Heartbreak kills, or does it?

I've had my fair share of heartbreaks. Heartbreaks that taught me so much. Heartbreaks that transformed me. Heartbreaks that remained at the back of my mind, even as I got to meet new people. Heartbreaks that haunted me each night. Heartbreaks that I got over quickly – they were still heartbreaks, even if they didn't last as long as those that came before them, or those that arrived after.

The reason for this is because I categorise heartbreaks in the following manner:

i. *Facetious heartbreaks* – heartbreaks that *you presume* are heartbreaks but aren't when you look back after a few months.

ii. *Friendship heartbreaks* – heartbreaks that involve unrequited feelings from one friend towards the other.

iii. *Nearly-there heartbreaks* – heartbreaks where that person could have been the one, but it didn't work out and as time goes on, you realise *why* they weren't the one.

iv.   *Painful heartbreaks* – they *feel* like they're more real than the others. They are the tenderest. The ones that cause a tumultuous stir in your journey. The ones that you take forward with you for most of your life. The ones that change you forever.

There are a few differences between the categories above; the intensity of pain, the duration of moving on, the level of growth, the change that the heartbreak brings about in your life and the knowledge that it imparts.

When you think about it, your heart can get injured for a variety of reasons, it doesn't always need to be a result of losing the one that you love. Your heart gets hurt when you lose a friend. Your heart gets hurt when someone close to you acts in a horrible way towards you. Your heart gets hurt when things don't go the way you wanted them to. Your heart gets hurt when reality doesn't coincide with the dreams that you'd created for yourself. And, of course – your heart gets hurt when it doesn't work out with the person whom you felt you truly loved.

When you experience heartbreak, it's as real as any other. In the same way when you love someone, it feels just as real as the first time, the second, or the third.

Heartbreaks differ in the degree of pain. Of course – it's up to you whether you want to categorise one as a heartbreak and not the other because of the amount of distress that it caused you. But that doesn't mean that the one before this heartbreak, or the one after this one isn't going to be as real as the one that you're experiencing right now. It's still real – it just may be more, or less, significant depending on the impact it has on your life.

Often, we tell ourselves that heartbreaks destroy us completely. They break us down and it's extremely difficult to come through from them and find ourselves again. But recently I've developed a fresh perspective on heartbreaks – every time your heart breaks, you truly come alive. This is because – time after time – whenever it looked like my life was completely falling apart, that's when it was slowly coming together. It hasn't happened once, or twice, but time and time again.

This makes me think that perhaps we view heartbreaks a little too harshly.

The truth is – none of us want to get our heart broken. It's the worst. It causes you undeniable agony. You can't focus on anything else in your life because you're profoundly consumed by this one incident. It's not pleasant and I don't wish it upon any of you. But when you think about, you would come across the following revelation – if we didn't break our hearts then how would we become stronger? How would we recognise what is good or bad for us? How would we distinguish between friendship, infatuation and love?

If we endorse the categories of heartbreak that I've provided above, then we are bound to get our hearts broken – and broken badly – before we learn whom to trust and whom not to. You see, episodes in our lives deliver invaluable wisdom to us and it's not just the feeling of love that shows us what love is, *it is also the feeling of heartache.* Crying on the hands of someone who didn't love us enough, or back, or honestly can show us *what love should and shouldn't be.*

If our hearts didn't break, we wouldn't realise that we were denying ourselves of self-love. If our hearts didn't break, we wouldn't know that we were settling for less than what we deserved. If our hearts didn't break, we wouldn't come to terms with whether we truly loved someone or whether it was merely an infatuation. If our hearts didn't break, we wouldn't be able to distinguish between the love that we want and the love that we're entitled to and how – sometimes they overlap but often they don't and, more often than not, the love that is meant for us is the one that will bring the most amount of positivity in our lives. And never that much discomfort.

If our hearts didn't break, then we wouldn't fall apart and come together again – in the way that we were truly meant to.

I want you to understand that even though heartbreaks are messy and bitter for your soul – they are vital instruments in the disordered pattern of life that we all experience. They show us what we need and what we should accept. They allow us to squeeze self-love and never put someone before ourselves in such a manner that it contravenes with our mental and emotional health. Heartbreaks can make us fall apart, but they also make us come together.

Heartbreaks can make us truly come alive.

Save Yourself

Have the strength to let go of people in order to save yourself.

Not everyone is going to be good for you, and sometimes you need to look at all the reasons why it won't work out rather than focusing on the one reason why it will and letting that lead you. The doubts that you have in the beginning become the reason why everything shatters in the end. And it's better to protect your heart rather than let it run wildly time and time again, causing itself grief.

Remember this – if someone is meant to be in your life, even if you let them go to protect yourself, they will come back at a time when they're good for you and you're good for them.

Don't force relationships. If it doesn't feel right, then let it be and know that whatever is destined for you will always find its way back to you. Have faith, because it will.

Until then – be there for yourself and take care of your heart.

Because it needs you to.

Excuses

Stop saying, *'It's okay, things will get better,'* after yet another argument.

Stop telling yourself that everything will be fine after yet another sleepless night where you've both gone to bed angry at each other. After one more day of wondering why your relationship keeps messing up, and why you're not as happy as you thought you would be, and why love isn't the warm, tender miracle that you imagined it was. To begin with – *love isn't a miracle* but that doesn't mean that it can't be sunny, silky and soft. All those dreams that you had for yourself – exist.

The love that you've hoped for will find its way to you. With the same magic in the air, the same chest-throbbing hugs, and the flutter in your stomach when you see them for the first time, with the same gradual changes where you go from chest flutters to a steady peace inside your soul when they are around. It all exists – but because you're so caught up in a relationship that doesn't serve you, *you fail to see it.*

Stop telling yourself that this is how relationships are every time you have a fight. Every time they hurt you or you hurt them. Every time that you go over the possibility of leaving them. Every time you stress or fret or get upset because you're frustrated at why your relationship isn't how you had envisioned. Your relationship should be what you want, especially since you put the hard work and care into it. And if it isn't, if you constantly find yourself pondering over other possibilities, if you're anxious, if you don't feel at home, if there are more bad days than good – then this relationship isn't for you.

Love is healthy and relationships aren't toxic or bad for you.

With the right person – love is truly an adventure and a relationship has the potential to be one of the best things that could happen to you. With the right person, you don't go to bed upset with each other, and even if you do, it's not to the point that it has a negative impact on your mental and emotional health. With the right person, you don't fight to a point that it becomes unhealthy. Yes, you argue. Yes, you have problems and disagreements. Yes, there will be differences – but that is how healthy relationships work. It's not always rainbows and sunshine, but it doesn't mess with your mind to such an extent that you can't think straight anymore.

With the right person, your goals look achievable, your value increases and the future looks beautiful and bright. With the right person, there's an abundance in your life and the air feels tender and warm.

Relationships aren't easy and that's the truth. They require dedication. Commitment. Sacrifice. They require making changes to your life. They require an understanding and loyalty and, sometimes, discomfort. But you take the best adventures in life when you step out of your comfort zone. This doesn't mean that relationships are lethal. It doesn't mean that the discomfort is permanent or unhealthy. It doesn't mean that just because you have to work hard in your relationship, that you can't be happy. Because that's not true.

The right love will be a combination of adventure, peace and challenges. It will be like a dream. The kind where you see yourself achieving and conquering but know how much they will demand of you. The dreams where you will have to invest a lot of time, energy and dedication but will bear the fruit of your hard work eventually. That is how you should view relationships.

Stop telling yourself that what you're experiencing right now is what love is when deep down your heart tells you otherwise.

Love isn't toxic. Love isn't unhealthy. Love isn't having to reassure yourself that you love them even though they cause you pain again and again. Love isn't any of those things. And once you recognise this truth – you will move away from all those feelings that are bad for you and move towards what's good. Only then will you let in what's truly meant for you.

Only then will you embrace a love that is truly deserving of *both of you.*

Walk Away

If you don't see respect reflecting in their eyes when they look at you, walk away. If your heart doesn't thump erratically in your chest the first time that you kiss, hug or hold hands, walk away. If picturing the future scares you more than excites you, if you can't imagine – *let alone plan* – your days, weeks or months ahead with them, walk away. If you know with certainty that you're bad for them or that they're bad for you and there's no way you can resolve this, walk away.

If you have tried to be better, to love them more, to allow both of you to grow, to give the relationship time, to be patient and kind and did whatever you had to do to keep the relationship going and it hasn't worked, walk away. If, when you initially fall for them, your heart doesn't say, *'Finally, there you are'*, walk away. If there's no loyalty, trust or companionship, walk away. If loving them hurts you, and not the way you'd expect, walk away. If you aren't becoming better versions of yourself, or at least progressing together, walk away.

Walk away from any relationship that doesn't serve you or them, because one day you will both find partners that you deserve, and you won't have to put all your energy in convincing yourself to stay.

Accept the Truth

Sometimes, the only reason why we hold on to people – even after they're gone – is because we are stuck on the idea of *'what could have been'* if we had just stayed together. We paint this attractive picture of how our relationship would have blossomed, had we just worked on it a little.

And this is self-destructive.

You're fixating on something that never happened to hold on to someone *who is long gone*. And the truth is, you don't know how your relationship may or may not have turned out because you two did not *live it out*. Instead, all you have is an idea of how your relationship may have been without experiencing it.

Sometimes you can't let go of someone because of your belief about *'how good'* you two would have been together, but you can't be sure of that. It could have gone well, yes, but it could have also gone badly. You need to learn that perhaps this was the best possible outcome. Perhaps you two not working out is a beautiful blessing in disguise – and that's the truth. Rather than pondering over *'what could have been'*, open your eyes to *what is* – and the truth is that you both didn't stay together because it wasn't meant to be. That's all.

And I hope you can accept this truth without letting it break you.

Moving on – what I learnt and the lessons I want to share with you.

Moving on is tough. It's unbelievably tough. Especially the first few weeks and months after you decide that you need to step away from this person and put yourself first. During my experience of moving on – I battled with several negative thoughts, a storm of emotions and, most importantly, denial. I will explain what I mean by *'denial'* later in this section, but for now I want us to peel off the first stage of moving on.

It is so unbelievably difficult.

You invest a certain amount of time in getting to know someone. Perhaps you end up becoming good friends and – unwillingly – you develop one-sided feelings for them over time. Or you both start falling for each other. Gradually, as time wears on, days turn into weeks and unfamiliarity meshes into something so profound that neither of you would've expected it. But it happens. Or you get into a relationship with them and fall head over heels in love. But it doesn't work out. Either they leave you or you leave them. And you're both devastated. You felt so strongly for them but now you've got nothing but memories and a lump the size of a huge rock grinding between your ribs where your heart had been.

How could this happen to you? How could it not work out?

You thought that they were the one. They were the person whom you were going to spend the rest of your life with. How, with the positive direction that your relationship was going in, did you take a U-turn? How can you find yourself exactly where you began – single, alone and, this time, with the prospect of never finding someone like that again? It doesn't make sense. It just doesn't.

That's why – moving on is one of the most difficult and heart-wrenching journeys that you will take.

Most of you already know, but for those of you who don't – your body replicates the physical manifestation of experiencing the death of someone. That's how brutally heartbreak hits you. Your palms get sweaty, your breath comes in quick abrupt bursts, your heartbeat races, you lose your appetite, your mind is whirring with horrible ideas, questions shoot at you from every corner and you sit there, simmering in grief and uncertainty. You have no idea how you're going to glue all these pieces laying by your feet and get on with your life as you were before they arrived.

Just for clarification – when I say moving on, I mean moving on from a variety of relationships, as I mentioned above. It could be a one-sided feeling-ship. It could be a fully-fledged relationship. It could be a dating-ship which lasted a few days, weeks or months. It could be a deep crush. If you're hurting, *you're hurting.* The intensity of the relationship that you shared with this person – whether they were your friend, someone you were dating or someone you were in a relationship with – isn't defined by the length of time you were together but by the strength of your feelings for them. By the impact that they had on you. By their presence in your life. That's what matters. Not the length of time that you were/were not together.

Simply put – you expend your energy, emotions and your life on them, only for it to not work out. Then, unwillingly, you pick up all the mess – bits of your heart, strands of memories, fragments of your interactions and all those emotions that pulled you towards them, as well as your hopes and dreams – and you begin the slow walk down the ambiguous road ahead.

Moving on is difficult when it's not what you wanted. Moving on is hard even when it's inevitable. Moving on is a weight that you carry on your shoulders when you felt that this relationship could have been the best thing that happened to you.

But read this: if you've decided to move on, then it clearly wasn't the best thing for you because if it was – *you both would (still) be together.*

Yes, it's hard to twist your head back one last time to look at the person who brought unlimited sunshine into your life. It's incredibly painful to let yourself untangle in slow motion from the person with whom you had a future planned. And it's going to be the most uneven, rocky ride that you ever take from hereon. But this is what's right for you, and deep down – *no one knows it better than you do.*

So, after you make the tough, yet essential, decision to move on – what happens next?

Aside from the sleepless nights, emptiness and itching loss – *you experience denial.* Denial happens when you refuse to identify the muggy reality that you're in after you break up – again, more broadly this means from a relationship, a friendship or a dating-ship. Instead of embracing the truth that it's over and, perhaps, you're the one that ended it – you grip fervently onto the dreams that you had when they were in your life. You secretly wish that they change their mind and apologise, or give you closure (if you haven't gotten it already) or even ask you to remain friends.

If, on this occasion, you were the one that ended the relationship with them, you're still in denial about what might happen next. Even though you don't realise it, you might have made the decision to break it off with the intention of scaring them. Maybe you didn't want to break up but had to because of the direction the relationship was headed. Or it happened by accident. You wanted to push their buttons and you ended up blurting out words that you didn't mean. And now you're alone; grieving a relationship that you never wanted to leave behind to begin with.

My response to this is simple – if you had a solid reason to call it off, you've already boarded the boat of setting sail from that relationship, no matter what your incentive was. If you thought that you need to scare them in order to get them to *'act right'*, then there was something inherently wrong with the relationship. And it's for this reason that you're in this place. The possibility of them realising everything that was wrong with their approach to the relationship *is very low*. But let's accept for a moment that it's high. Perhaps they will come back, and you have a glimmer of faith. But if days and weeks have passed, then it's more likely that this person will come to terms with all the mistakes they made *after* you've moved on. By then it will be too late for them. Because no matter what they will say/do – you won't let them back into your life.

During denial, thoughts of going back to them or letting them return hammer inside your mind. Hard. Especially in the first 6 months-1 year of moving on. If they come back during this period and don't offer any solutions or improvement in behaviour – *you will still take them back into your life.* Because your brain hasn't fully registered that the relationship/friendship is over.

As I said earlier, during a heartbreak your brain replicates the physiology of *literally losing someone* (i.e. death). Denial is a huge part of grief after someone's death. You look over old photos and a lingering smile hugs your lips. You recall past conversations – technology makes this easier as we now have every conversation saved and backed up on our phones/laptops/the beautiful cloud in the sky. Your mind refuses to let you grasp that they're gone. They're going to come back one day. This is all a huge nightmare and it will be over before you know it.

This is how your mind works in the first stage of moving on.

You refuse to admit that it's over, or even if you slowly come to terms with it – your heart is still where it was a few weeks/months ago; *with them*. If they were to come back to you with it, you would accept them instantly. You might even introduce a few face-value rules to convince yourself and them that you're serious about making a positive change in your relationship. But you both will inevitably forget about those rules after a few weeks of being together again. And the previous toxic patterns will follow. This also applies when someone who led you on for months or years returns to your life. Or, if you're like me and have weak willpower, *you might even return to them.*

I am guilty. I'm guilty for letting the course of denial push me back to a one-sided feeling-ship with a friend, knowing with certainty at the back of my mind that they would never like me. All I was doing was delaying the process of me moving on, rather than putting a stop to those doomed emotions and cutting the uncomfortable friendship short. That's the difficulty with moving on. In the beginning, your denial will have you believe anything – even the rare, near-impossible idea that this person will change their mind about you. That, this time it will be different. This time distance would have shown them exactly what they were missing out by rejecting your love.

If you were in a one-sided feeling-ship with someone; here's what I have to say about letting them back into your life – *don't do it.*

Being friends with someone whom you have one-sided feelings for isn't a good idea to begin with. To add to it, if they do any of the following then they haven't *earned your friendship either*: they lead you on, engage in careless banter, flirt with you or get close to you to the point where you're ruthlessly attached only to eventually tell you that they don't like you back. If they were sensitive to your emotions and knew that you liked them *(oh, they knew)*, they would've told you straight away that it was never going to work, and you should move on.

Once you've made the decision to leave them – *well done, I'm proud of you* – it would be futile to be *'just friends'* again, no matter how much time has passed. Unless you or they are suddenly in a relationship (and not a rebound one) and you're certain – *truly certain,* not fake certain – that you've moved on for good and your feelings for them won't arise.

I speak from experience, so, just trust me – even if weeks pass, even if 6 months pass, even if a year passes and you're both still single, if they return to your life and want to be your *'friend'*, hope that they might like you back will light up inside you like a Christmas tree – the one that dwindled when you decided to remove them from your life. With full force. Brighter than before because all those whimsical ideas of *'Meant to be'*, and *'If it comes back to you, it's yours'*, will roam around your mind like white birds circling around cartoon character's heads after they bang them, while your eyes are swirling with love– indicating that you've lost all sense.

Let me go into more detail.

In your reunion as friends, you will both return to the same pattern of throwing flirtatious lines back and forth, giggling with each other, talking endlessly until you get attached to each other once more, only for them to tell you after a few months that you are still *just friends'*, thrusting you back into the same dark pit that you're in right now.

Don't do it. Just don't. Don't let denial rule your mind.

Be strong during those first few weeks and months. And if they come back into your life and want to be *just friends'* – **say no**.

Secondly, for those of you who were in a relationship/dating-ship with someone and are moving on from the break-up – denial will try its best to direct you back to them. Denial will creep up on you on stretched, lonely nights when you're scrolling through Instagram and come across photos of more loved-up couples than you can deal with. It will instigate you when your cousins, friends and colleagues are getting into new relationships, getting married, making babies and moving on in their lives the way that you were going to. It will pound in your heart when you read over past WhatsApp messages when they uttered words like, *'trust'*, *'future'*, *'serious'* and *'love'*.

Denial will haunt you. It will bother you. It will try its best to convince you to change your mind – but it's up to you to not let it. It's up to you to remain firm – scrunch your hands into balls, look at your reflection in the mirror and affirm your decision of moving on. Tell yourself as clearly as you can that you're worth much more than what you were receiving from this relationship, and one day you will fall head over heels in love and everything that you've ever wanted from a relationship – and more –will come true for you.

Remember, *this is not a general rule.*

I'm not saying that it's never a good idea to reunite with someone after you break up with them. All I'm saying is that you shouldn't do it when you're in the *denial phase* – the one that pushes you to the brink of irrationality where, even if your relationship could have been saved, if you get back together during this period; it most probably won't survive.

The reason for that is as follows: if you broke up with someone and somehow you both evolve in wonderful ways, albeit apart, and decide to reunite once more – then that's great. The time away from them shaped you. It made you resilient. You formed positive ideas about what you want from a relationship and this time – when you both get together – you will have reasonable expectations from each other. This time round, you will approach your relationship through a wiser lens.

If they come back to you or you decide to go back to them after a while apart where you've grown and realised *your mistakes* as well as *theirs*, when you reunite – both of you will try to do *everything right* to make it work. You won't fall back into your old toxic patterns. You won't take each other for granted. You won't get lazy. And even if you do – you will have developed the necessary tools to deal with it. This time *you will work hard*. Really hard.

You will try your best to make it work.

Most people don't go back to their ex and most people's exes don't come back to them. This is another truth that you must grasp during the denial stage – *they're not coming back*. And you can't make them. Hold your head high and your shoulders higher and admit to yourself that this may be the end of your relationship.

For others – the ones *who can* save their relationship – you need to understand that the *'reunion'* with your partner might happen after many months or even years. That is invaluable grieving and healing time that you could use to promote your wellbeing and health and to cultivate as a person. Don't let it pass you by just like that. Use this precious time to do some essential self-work. Read books. Learn a new language. Join the gym. Establish a new hobby or return to hobbies that you had prior to the relationship. Spend time with your family and friends. Get pampered. Go on a holiday – the world is your oyster. Or do nothing, nothing at all – if that's what makes you truly happy.

The first stage after a break-up is significant, and you could do so much with it. Remember that the choice is yours and yours only.

But don't let them come back – or go back to them – when you're in the denial stage. Nothing good comes out of getting back with your ex after an instant or serious breakup. You won't be ready to talk about the stuff that hurts. You won't be willing to look inwards at your own mistakes and point out theirs. You won't want to fix stuff because your mind will still be clouded with the misery that their absence left. All you will want is them. *Back.* It won't matter what they did wrong and it won't matter if they don't give you a meaningful apology. Neither of you will discuss your problems until another few months – or year – down the line where perhaps *it will end badly again.*

Take my advice and be as strong as you can during the denial stage of moving on. Delete their number if you must. Block them on social media. Remove yourself from WhatsApp groups and stop talking to their friends. Do whatever it takes – but don't go back to them. Not yet, anyway.

Earlier I said that I'll speak about what I learnt from my own experiences, and perhaps the most vital insight that I gained from moving on is this – *I can survive anything.*

And if you don't agree with me, then recall the number of times you've been wounded in the past. Remember when you were at school and had a crush on someone in your class and they made fun of you. Or they liked you back, but they moved to a different area and left school altogether. Or they told your friend that they liked him/her instead – leaving your very first crush incomplete. Then you grew up a bit, now a teenager, and went through several changes – one of them being that you could have *'those kind'* of feelings for other people. Maybe it didn't work out and the first time you truly liked someone – it didn't work out. Or it did, and you got into your first relationship as a 14/15-year old. But you broke up within 6 months and cried over a tub of ice-cream with your best friend while watching The Notebook or played COD all night long with your friends while repeating, *'Girls ain't shit'* to yourself.

Remember your first heart break. Then your second. And the one after that. Throughout your life, you've had the good fortune to meet new people time and time again. People who made you smile and laugh. People who impacted your outlook on life. People who introduced you to new music, art and lifechanging books that stayed with you even after they left.

People whom you fell in love with and people who fell in love with you. People who changed your life forever.

Each time, it felt like the end of the world when it was over. The next time was worse than the previous. Then, after a few months or a year, you woke up and realised that the heavy weight that was on your heart had vanished. You smiled and, this time, it crinkled up at the corners of your eyes and spread throughout your body, tingling your insides with warmth. With softness. You got dressed to see your friends and, as you sat in a private booth at your favourite diner, one of your friends told a characteristic joke. A joke that they'd told for as long as you had known them and – for the first time in months – you laughed. It was a real, guttural laugh that vibrated through your body, and when you threw your head back, you understood for the first time in a long time – your heart was finally mending.

You knew at that moment, and perhaps had known it from all your previous experiences, that time heals all wounds. And you returned to normal life not long after that and, even if you didn't return to your old self, you turned into someone new. Into someone stronger. Then someone else came along unexpectantly and turned your life over once more. For better or for worse. But you kept falling. Kept giving parts of your heart away. Kept letting go of old pieces and welcoming new ones. You kept grasping more truths and evolving. You kept growing.

The same cycle of falling, hurting and healing have encompassed so many of our lives. Every time it happens, you think that you won't move on from it. Every time, you tell yourself that this time *it felt too real*. This time *it killed like never before*. This time *I can't move on from it*. But you do. *You do*. And this is what I want you all to take forward with you.

Moving on taught me about the chaotic, but similar pattern of so many of our lives. How, everyone you meet will contribute to your growth and sometimes they stay – but most of the time they leave for you to adapt without them. For you to become the person you were meant to be. Moving on taught me about my strength. I kept thinking, *'This time, it's too real'*, *'This time, I won't be able to move on'*, repeatedly until I got over it. I kept telling myself, *'My heart hasn't hurt this badly'*, until, a year or two down the line, my heart was whole and bursting with more love than I knew what to do with. Moving on taught me that there's nothing I can't survive. And this is the only truth that I take forward with me.

I know what you're thinking, *'You moved on, so it means you didn't truly love them'*.

And I'm not sure how to answer that question other than with this – at the time, *it felt like a lot like love*. At the time, I could *feel* the pain physically searing through me every moment I breathed, as though the agony was throbbing inside my chest. At the time, my mental health declined, my dreams fell out of the window, tears leaked down my cheeks every night for months and months and I couldn't find an escape. At the time, it felt like my world was over. Looking back, I don't know how, when or why – but I survived. I moved on. And you will too. Moving on doesn't mean that it wasn't love. At least not when you were in it. Moving on doesn't mean that what you felt wasn't real.

Your definition of love is bound to mould with time. The concepts that you form stem from an accumulation of the chapters in your life. What you know of love will change significantly, regardless of whether you stay with the same person or not. But you won't realise this until you move on. And the only way to do this is to bundle up strength into your fists and wrap your wrists with the string of self-love. The only way to do this is to drink up the truth that it might hurt for a little while – *but in the end it will be worth it.*

Don't let the same toxicity back into your life.

No matter how much you want them. No matter how lonely you feel. No matter how much you miss them. No matter what anyone says or does. Don't let your mind become weak. Trust me, you will make it.

You will survive this. You will find love.

The first step to moving on in your life is to close old chapters, lock the door and throw away the key. If those people are meant to be in your life – they might return at a time when they're good for you and you're good for them. But for now, focus on yourself. Affirm your existence and know that everything that you want from your life – you will achieve.

You can do it. I have faith in you.

Chasing Love

You can't fight to be loved by someone.

If someone genuinely cares about you and wants you in their life, they will do whatever it takes to keep you there. If you're confused about how they feel, if they pull you in only to push you away, if what they say troubles your mind or makes you feel misunderstood – then you must let them go. Actions speak louder than words and if you can't see love or care for yourself in their eyes, the truth is that it probably isn't there. I know that you want to give them the benefit of doubt; they need time, you're pushing them too much, or you both should take it slow – all these possibilities are valid, but they don't apply in cases where you're not sure about your place in someone's life.

It's fine to take extra time if you're both headed in the same direction. It's okay to walk slowly on this journey if you both want to get to know each other as friends before anything else. But if they confuse you or give you mixed signals, or if they treat you right only to treat you badly again – then they're bringing negative energy into your life which is not okay. Trust me when I tell you that you can't chase love or care. Because if you must force love – then it is never going to be love.

Heartbreak

Heartbreaks really do kill. They do. You tell yourself that you will never come through from what you're experiencing because nothing could feel worse than this. Nothing could hurt you as much as the person – whom you love dearly – leaving you does. Nothing could pound inside your heart more than loneliness does. *But it does get better.* The sun shines once more. The pain slowly starts to fade and the person whom you thought you couldn't live without becomes a distant memory that disappears far into your past.

When your heart breaks, it's like your whole world is falling apart but in reality – that's when your whole world finally comes together. That's when you realise who is meant for you and who isn't. That's when you cherish your worth and appreciate that sure, love isn't easy, but it was never what you thought it would be to begin with. That's when you're able to grasp that love is not harmful, angry or fierce, love does not bang a door on your face or ignore the palm that you stretched out for them to take in theirs. Love does not embarrass you. Love does not make you feel small. Love is not selfish, rude or unsure about where to place you in their life. Love does not make you cry or question what you deserve.

But you don't know this when you're pining for them. You don't know this when you can't see beyond the horrible cycle that you find yourself in. So, believe me when I tell you that *them leaving* is what *builds you*. Them leaving gives you a newfound purpose. Them leaving allows you to be free once more and fly towards what's meant for you. Them leaving opens doors, opportunities and adventures that you would've never had if they were here. Them leaving returns you back to yourself, where you always belonged. Heartbreak may hurt you, but it doesn't destroy your world – because, over time – it makes your world slowly come together.

People Leave

Sometimes people leave, not because they weren't meant to stay in your life but because they needed to leave for you to realise how invaluable they were. You see, it's not always about the other person gaining knowledge or flourishing as a result. Sometimes, you're the one who needs to learn to adapt and admit your mistakes.

And it is okay.

It's okay to recognise that you hurt someone, as long as you've now understood how to make a positive change to the way that you treat people. It's okay to make mistakes, as long as the experiences following those mistakes have taught you how to rectify them. And it's okay to realise what you lost after someone leaves. As long as the next time round, when something like this occurs, you will know what you could do better. Because it's not about pining over what you lost because you can't change the past and bring them back. It's about learning from your mistakes and trying to be a good person. Sometimes people leave because we need to grasp a vital truth about life, and it's okay.

Rather than regretting what you did that made them walk away, focus on whoever comes after them – and what (if you truly want them in your life) you could do to make them stay.

Let Go

Often, the biggest lesson you can receive is knowing when to let go. It's so difficult to do – to look at someone who makes you incredibly happy, but also causes you undeniable pain and say, *'I am moving on from you'*. But it's an action that you need to take if you care about yourself. It doesn't matter how happy they make you. If they are also the cause of your sorrow, then you must leave and not return until you can be *just happy* in their presence. This isn't to say that they can't bring you sorrow, but if there isn't an abundance of happiness and *there is an abundance of pain* – then you need to leave in order to save yourself. If you can never be *just happy* with them by your side, if pain will always follow – and outweigh – the happiness that they bring, then you need to accept that this was as far as this person was meant to stay in your life.

Often, the most beautiful lessons are the hardest, and leaving is the most difficult out of the rest to do. But to love yourself, you need to learn to let go of those who can't give you the happiness that belongs with you.

People Let You Down

Don't associate your happiness with a single person or object. Everyone and everything is contingent and the only truth that you can be sure of is this – even when everyone else leaves, you will still be there.

I spent most of my life tying myself to others. Then my heart got injured. Once. Then again. And again. After all that time, I told myself firmly that I'm not going to put the weight of my happiness on other people – because I need to find happiness within myself.

That's the thing about people.

They weave into your life with promises of *'love'* and *'forever'* dripping off their lips like honey. They convince you that they're different and that they won't let you down with words such as, *'Trust me, I will never hurt you'*. And as a result, you witness your high walls crumbling slowly, brick by brick, until you let them into your soul. Entirely. Until you give them more than you've given to anyone before. That's the thing about people. Often, the words that slither out of their mouth don't match their actions. They make promises and end up breaking them, leaving you alone – once more – with another scrape across your chest and a sharp emptiness pounding within. And once more, even though others let you down – you feel like you're the one who let yourself down by trusting them.

Closure

Maybe, you will get your closure. Maybe, you will receive your apology, and the person – for whom pain rattled inside your heart for a long time – will realise what they did wrong and run back to you for forgiveness. For another chance. To make amends. To be lovers again. Or to remain friends. But you can't wait around for this to happen. You can't walk ahead with the shackle of the past forced around your ankle. Because what if they don't come back? What if you don't get the apology/closure that you deserve? What if realisation doesn't hit them like a brick and they continue to live their life the way they always have?

You can't be sure of anyone but yourself. Especially not those who have let you down before. Please just *let it be*. Peel off the past like an old, shabby coat that can't keep you warm anymore, and put on the jumper of healing – the velvety, warm one that has comforted you more than once in the past.

Don't fret about whether they will return. Don't scrutinise what could or should happen. Focus on *what is* the case and let them go. Let them be. It's not worth it. Not because that's what they deserve, but because that's what you deserve.

Effort

If someone cares about you, they will make time for you. You won't sit there and wonder what you mean to them because they haven't replied to your messages. You won't lose sleep over the way they treat you – hot one day and cold the next. You won't fret or worry about whether they will change their mind and leave you. You will just know, because they will be honest about their feelings. They will reply to your text messages with just as much enthusiasm as they did the first time. They will always be on the other end of the phone, and if they can't be then they will let you know that even though they're busy – they're still thinking of you. They will treat you with just as much love and care as you give them. And they will never leave you wondering. You will never be confused about what your place in their life is.

If someone cares about you, the amount of effort that they put into you won't decrease once you're together. In fact, it will get deeper, stronger and more consistent. If someone really cares about you, they will never leave you feeling empty or unloved.

Believe me, they won't.

You Deserve Love

We spend so long believing that the person who left us behind was the one who was meant for us that we fail to see all the reasons why it wouldn't have worked, all the reasons why *it didn't work*. Sure, it's horrible when you lose the one that you love. It's the worst when they were the first person you ever loved – but love changes over time. So does what is right for you. So does what is kind and considerate to your heart and not the clutter that you found yourself in when you loved them.

Because if they were meant for you – they wouldn't have cracked you open and taken all that was yours. If they were meant for you, you wouldn't have lost yourself in the process of trying to string together the shreds that they left behind. If they were meant for you, they would have been healthy for your soul. You wouldn't be searching for your missing pieces after they left, because they would have filled your heart to the point where even their departure would have left you feeling whole.

If they were meant for you, they would be here right now but they're not.

So sure, they might find someone who is wonderful, kind and full of love – *but you will find your person too*. The person whose smile is enough to light up all that has dimmed inside you. The person who holds your hand to never take a step in the other direction without asking if you will be okay, *because they care*. Because they want you to be happy. Because they value your heart as the gem that it is. You will find the person who regards your dreams higher than you do, and who pours so much of themselves into you that you're more than whole, you feel like two people are living inside one, you feel like you've never felt before because *this is what love is supposed to look like.*

Everything that you've dreamt of does come true, but only with the right person. With the one who has the intention to love you. With the one who knows how important you are. With the one who is meant for you – because whoever came before them wasn't right.

Believe in this truth the next time you see your past walk in front of you. Because the person who is meant for you will find every grain of magic within you – the kind of magic that you never knew existed. And this person will be wonderful too. They will be so wonderful to you.

Because you deserve love. You do. *You do.*

The first time that I broke my heart.

We were best friends for 6 years before we met each other.

No, we didn't live in the dark ages. We could have met if we wanted to but neither of us expressed an interest, and we were both fine with it. We went about our lives and chatted consistently on MSN, Bebo and BBM before moving on to WhatsApp – our friendship growing along with our online forms of communication. Sometimes we'd lose contact for a few months before resuming our friendship again, and we'd pick up exactly where we left it a few months ago.

During our friendship, we both liked other people. He even had a girlfriend (or a few) for a short while. I never got into a relationship in the time that I'd known him – but that's a story for another book.

This went on for years until we finally decided to meet up as friends. I mean, it was high time. We'd become such good friends for so long. Our young teenage and adolescent years were spent sharing secrets and jokes and being there for each other through all the highs and lows that being a teenager brings with it. But looking back – I realised that I was the one who did most of the talking. I was the one who shed off more about myself than he ever did. I told him my secrets. I revealed my vulnerabilities. I expressed my fears and insecurities. I was honest. Upfront. Raw. But he was none of those things.

But being this honest is a core personality trait of mine. I always give more than I receive without foreseeing the disastrous consequence that this will have on my friendships/relationships. Because if you're giving more than the other person – *then you're bargaining to lose more as well.*

Anyway, back to my friend; he wasn't expressive, nor – upon reflection – was he my type. He was a good friend. He would make me laugh, I could pass time with him, exchanging jokes on WhatsApp for hours and we could have meaningless chats about literally anything – but that's as far as it went. That's why the years had passed, and I never developed any strong feelings for him. At least not until I was 21. *I had liked* him over the years. But it was more of an innocent *he-is-my-only-guy-friend* kind of crush.

So, we finally decided to meet for the first time when I was 20.

I don't know how else to describe it other than it being the most awkward first meeting of my life. I didn't get it. It wasn't like I was meeting a stranger. We'd been friends for *6 whole years* already. We had a solid friendship and we practically knew everything about each other *(or so, I thought)* – how could it feel this awkward? But it did. When I first in his car, I instantly felt anxious – as though I was sitting beside a stranger. Our banter was dry, our small talk was forced and the conversations that we shared were tinged with the same dullness that you'd expect from a first meeting with someone you barely knew. Overall, we had an *okay* time that day, and I returned home and reminded myself why he was only my friend and *nothing more.*

But a few events took place after that. Incidents that I won't go into too much detail about, but there I was, 7 months later – at 21 – crying over the same guy I'd had one friendly date with *in 7 years.*

Let me just clarify one thing – I'm not trying to downplay our friendship. Because even though we only met once, throughout the years he became a pivotal part of my life. Perhaps the previous generations won't be able to comprehend this, but as millennials living in an everchanging technological world, we take our *'online'* friendships just as seriously as our face-to-face friendships, if not more. We depend on phone calls and WhatsApp messages to check in on each other, ticking it off our *'mental list of interactions'* scheduled for that week. We pen in a call for a few days or a week later to have a quick catch up.

We meet some of our closest friends *only once* every few months because we're all so *'busy'* in our lives. But whenever we do meet, not much has changed in terms of our love for each other.

We catch up, share gossip, rewind into each other's lives and depart with a promise on our lips that we will meet sooner next time. But that doesn't happen. Our next meeting is just as far apart, if not more, than our previous one. But this doesn't bother us too much. Because we regularly exchange messages, we check each other's latest Instagram photos, follow stories and witness each other's holidays online, and text or call in between. Through social media our interactions pace forward steadily. Because gadgets allow us to maintain social relationships without the effort of physical engagement, and it works fine for us.

It's for this reason that I'm certain you will understand what I mean when I say that he was one of my closest friends, even though we'd barely met over the 7 years that we'd known each other.

Anyway, back to my story; *the year 2015 was significant.* Not only was it the first time that I'd meet him alone (that friendly, yet awkward date), but it was also the year where our friend groups would collide. It meant that I saw him more than I had in all those years combined – *even if it was in the presence of others.* It was also the year that I would lose him as a friend forever.

After growing up together, when our friendship fell apart and I lost him – I lost a part of me too.

I told myself that I loved him.

Why else would my heart hurt this much?

Why else would I be crying myself to sleep each night, after what happened, if I didn't love him?

Why else would I feel this lonely, *this empty,* this vacant – as though a huge chunk of myself had been ripped off?

It had to be love. That was the only explanation.

And – to be honest – it was love at the time. It was love for *what I knew love to be love,* which is a fraction of *what I know love is now.* I had never been in a relationship. I hadn't gone on a single date. I'd never even gone on a date *with him* before concluding that I loved him. So, as you can see – my idea of *'love'* was limited. It was based on the innumerable Bollywood movies that I watched, the music I heard and the books I read – all painting love as a crimson, despairing affair with a tragic ending. To add to it, I didn't have a steady model of love to follow in my family either – my mother had passed away when I was young and my father's second marriage turned me further away from love and relationships rather than towards it.

But, of course, just like any other millennial who read too many romance novels, I thought that my story would be different. I believed that I was that special damsel in distress who was destined to get her happy ending.

In all honesty – *I was living in a fantasy world.*

I assumed that the first person I'd give my heart to would be the person that I marry (I know, *how unrealistic?)* and when that didn't happen, when reality didn't conform to the dreams that I'd created in my mind – it completely broke me.

How could this person, no matter how wrong he was for me,

not be 'the one'? I'd experienced so much in my life already. I'd witnessed too much pain, *too much anguish,* too much of everything that someone my age shouldn't have had to go through. And the least that God could do for me was give me my happily-ever-after.

Let me clarify that I'm not trying to devalue what I went through in my heartbreak because – *it was hell.*

The first year passed by in clutches of low mood, anxiety and dark thoughts. I didn't get help because I didn't think that I needed it. Instead, I tormented my cousins and close friends with hours of conversations where I teared up, complained and nodded my head to their rebuttals, followed by more tears before snapping the phone shut. Then it was just me and an unending, aching night until I would wake up the next morning and do it all over again. Somehow, I forced my way through the initial 6 months of throbbing heartache somehow. I felt like my heart had been ripped out of my chest and shredded into pieces. To top it off, those pieces had been stomped all over by someone whom I had trusted blindly.

I was certain that I could never be happy again.

I refused to consider the possibility of falling in love or welcoming someone else into my life. The mere idea of moving on from this person gave me anxiety. I couldn't do it. I just couldn't.

I was low, so low that I spent all my free time crying to myself in my room. I refused to take the handful of steps down the stairs to spend time with my family. And even when I did slope down those leaden steps to be in their company – my mind was in a different place altogether. I couldn't smile or laugh wholeheartedly. Whenever I felt okay, the inkling that something was wrong, silently niggling away at the back of my mind, would return – making me feel uneasy again.

I would share my writing online, talking about the possibility of moving on and being happy again, while dabbing at my own damp cheeks. And here's the weird thing about the whole situation – *I truly believed it.* I believed that it would all be okay for everyone *but me.* I had faith that God had a plan for everyone who was going through heartbreak, except me. Because nothing would never be okay *in my life again.*

How could it be okay?

How could it, when each morning was harder than the one before?

How could it, when my heart jarred against my ribcage, reminding me with every pressing second how heavy it felt?

How could it, when nothing felt right anymore? My dreams. My goals. My future. My soul.

There was a hard ball in my chest where my heart sat, and as time wore on, the biting chains of my heartbreak made each step in moving on more difficult than the previous.

I stopped combing my hair. My skin was horrible – I'd never suffered from such awful acne before. Makeup was a necessity to cover up the fat, red spots that developed all over my skin and I only put jeans on if I *had to* – I didn't even *bother* changing into them if I was going out alone or to the grocery store where the possibility of bumping into someone that I knew was high.

My life was deteriorating in every angle and it couldn't get any worse than this.

Then *'denial'* followed – the one that I told you all about earlier. The one where you convince yourself that this is all a huge mistake and they will come back to you soon to confess how wrong they were. I, too, thought that he would come back. He would realise all his mistakes and beg for me to accept him. At one point, I truly believed that I would change his mind. I hoped, no, *I knew* that he would realise how much he loved me, and we'd forget that any of this ever happened. And this conviction kept me going for the first 6 months. But the denial period went out of the window when I finally got my closure.

All it took was for him to look me in the eye and utter the words, *'It's never going to happen. There are much more important issues in my life for me to worry about than this* ***thing'.*** After this, I shoved him, and the denial, out of my system forever.

Something clicked in place that day. I don't know what it was. Perhaps the nonchalant expression on his face, or the way he kept shaking his leg and glancing at his watch, as if I was wasting his time. And maybe I was. Maybe I was wasting *both his and my time.* And I wasn't aware of this then but would fall face-flat into this truth years later.

Whatever it was, when I stepped out of his car that day – *I was free.*

I knew then that my heart wouldn't yearn for him ever again, because he never deserved it to begin with. Inevitably, he would realise his mistake after 2 years and come running back with an apology – they all do. But the day I received my closure, I decided that even if he came back, he wasn't going to get an inch of my heart after it healed.

After the closure came a rush of anger. The detesting. The, 'How dare he do this to me?', 'Who does he think he is?', and 'I'll show him'.

A bulb had finally lit up inside me. And in the months after me yearning for someone who wasn't worth an ounce of my tears, I found the purpose that I'd lost during my heartbreak. I remembered my dreams, the ones that I'd taken a huge risk for already. It was then that I decided to focus my attention back on what really mattered – my goals.

It's weird. My anger motivated me more than my initial passion for writing had. I mean, don't get me wrong – I loved writing from the bottom of my heart for as long as I could remember. But that was fiction. It was storytelling. Creating stories from nothing but my imagination was a passion of mine for as long as I could remember. But my heartbreak fuelled a passion of writing to heal in such a way that it transformed my life forever.

I felt rejected, and this rejection pushed me to prove myself – to me more than anyone. I had to feel confident and remind myself where my place was in the world. It was time to turn my focus back on the dreams that had ignited fire into my soul for so many years before my heartbreak.

Most importantly, I had to re-learn how to love myself.

All the rage that I felt until that point – I turned it outwards. I transformed it into a light so bright that it couldn't be ignored. I let the rage push me to create art. I wrote and wrote and wrote. I wrote until my heart felt lighter and the water on my cheeks dried into words on paper. I wrote until the twinge between my ribs subsided. Until every emotion that I had buried behind a wall came gushing out.

Writing healed me in more ways than I can express. Because through writing about my heartache and, subsequently healing from it, I learned a lot. Such as how the loneliness that follows a heartbreak can be deathly. And how you don't know someone until you see their darkness, and how important it is to never put the bulk of your life's happiness on anyone other than yourself. Lastly, I learnt what it means to give your heart to people. I learnt to value my heart a lot more after that, keeping it close to me, hidden and locked away in a chest that I stashed somewhere deep inside – a place where only the one that truly loved me would be able to get to.

My first heartbreak was the worst because it broke me completely. But the woman that I became after that – as I joined those pieces back together, as well as added new ones – *was incredible*. And I say this with utmost humbleness.

You see, I was merely existing before I broke my heart, but after it – *I was soaring*.

I developed direction and understood what it means to love myself, in a way that wasn't dependant on someone else loving me. Although there were countless questions buzzing like angry bees in my mind – which I would eventually get the answers to years down the line – throughout my healing journey I understood the importance of answering those questions for myself. I also embraced the value of forgiving and moving on, even if the person who broke you didn't ask for it. Because forgiveness is what we do for ourselves. Forgiveness is a tool for us – through which we're able to lift the weight of all the negativity that's still left inside our heart and move on for good.

Finally, I accepted that closure – just like forgiveness – *was only for me.*

Closure wasn't something that I could use to put a final word in. It wasn't a way to see him one last time so I would have more memories to hold on to – which would only cause me more discomfort in the long run. It wasn't a tool that I could use to change his mind or fix him. Closure was for me to get the answers that I was owed and if I didn't get those answers from him – then I had to find those answers for myself. Closure was for me, and me only.

In the same way – *closure is for you.*

Closure isn't there to give them a final chance to understand where they went wrong because, truthfully, the reason why everything turned this sour was because they *didn't understand.* They didn't realise how harsh their words were, how much of a mess they made, or the level of hurt that they caused. And perhaps they will never understand. But don't let this dishearten you.

Closure doesn't need to happen with the other person. They shouldn't have to sit you down and spit out stiff, leaden words with the hope that you will get the message. They shouldn't have to give you the ultimatum for you to understand that it's over. Because you can do that for yourself. You can give yourself closure. And this involves sitting yourself down to have that tough conversation. Uncovering the truth for yourself. Swimming deep into the pool of your thoughts to find your answers. Paying attention to your emotions and listening to what your heart needs – and giving it just that.

Following my heartbreak, I had innumerable experiences – ones that transformed me completely. I met new people with a different take on the world. I visited foreign places and read incredible books. I listened to uplifting music. I uncovered new cities and had wonderful adventures which provided me with a glimpse of how beautiful life could be.

All I had to do was embrace it.

Inevitably, when the person who broke my heart came back – he didn't find the girl that he'd left behind. We had grown. Separately. Apart. And it would take a whole lifetime to travel back to each other again if we wanted to. And, to be honest, *I didn't want to.* I was happy with the girl that I'd moulded into, and the woman that I was becoming. That time apart allowed me to unpick *'attachment'* and *'infatuation'* from *'love'* and *'commitment'.* I gained insight into all the practicalities of a relationship and – had we pursued it – the difficulties that would have befallen us. I agree that when you love someone – you're willing to go through every extent to make it work, and I will speak about this later. But we were never going to work.

And one major reason was that I no longer loved him.

I'm not sure if *I ever loved him to begin with* – not in the way that I appreciate love as now. It's possible that I was heavily infatuated and – because I didn't know better – I had the ill-founded conviction that he was the one. But he wasn't. He never had been. We'd always wanted different things. And I refused to admit it when I fell head over heels. I didn't accept that we would have never been happy together. Me, with my head lost in books and dreams in the soft pearls of my eyes as I soared towards the clouds with confidence that I would surpass them one day. And him, on the other end of the spectrum altogether.

I couldn't speak to him about what ignited me with passion. We never had intellectual conversations. He didn't take any interest in my dreams and I wasn't even aware of his. We didn't have a single conversation about what we wanted from our lives (respectively) in the 7 years that we'd been friends. We were children, that's all. And this is the only way that I can explain it.

It took breaking my heart for me to grasp that what I thought I wanted was far from what I truly deserved.

In the end, when I reached the peak of my healing and truly began to grow – after the denial, the closure and the hurdles – I was incredibly grateful for him impacting my life in the way he had. Because if he'd never hurt me, I wouldn't have become fierce or self-reliant. I wouldn't have learnt my worth. I wouldn't be where I am today. If he never broke my heart then I would have no idea what it was capable of, and how much love it had within it to give to others. I wouldn't have figured out my place in the world. I wouldn't have understood what was meant for me. I wouldn't have written away the pain. I wouldn't have realised what love is and what it isn't.

And in the end, I was – *I am* – grateful.

You might be thinking, *'How can you be grateful for someone cracking your heart open in more than one way?'* Because it did hurt. *It hurt like hell.* It tormented me for years and I lost pieces of myself that I will never find again. But *I don't want to* find those pieces. Those pieces were never supposed to stay with me to begin with. They didn't belong with who I was going to be – they don't belong with who I am today. Think about it this way – pieces of a jigsaw puzzle that don't fit together can be *forced* to fit together for a very small time, but the moment you remove that force from them; they will inevitably fall apart.

So, *I am grateful* for everything that I went through.

When we go through heartbreak – especially the initial stages – we can't see beyond the dark void that we find ourselves in. We don't have faith in any prospect of future contentment. But it exists. Beyond the emptiness. Beyond the dark, hollow tunnel. Beyond the cage of misery that entangles us during those early stages. We find our way eventually.

One day, you will reach a point in your life where you will be grateful for all the grief that they caused – because it built you. It shaped you into the warrior that you are today. It allowed you to see all the love inside your heart. You might not see it now, tomorrow or the day after – but one day you will. Take it from me. My first heartbreak allowed me to become the best version of myself – and for that, I am undeniably grateful.

Put You First

It's not that hard to drop a, *'I'm really sorry that I haven't replied. I'm busy but I'm still thinking of you'*, message to someone. It really isn't. And I hate it when people say that they're busy with work, family or friends which is why they couldn't get back to you – because these are all excuses. It's just a matter of priorities. Dropping one message takes less than 10 seconds, but it's enough to make another person's day.

You don't deserve someone who will message you after their night is over and they're *finally free to talk*. You deserve someone who will make time to message you while they're out with their friends, even if it's just to let you know that they might not be able to reply for a few hours but they're still here. You deserve someone who will check up on you throughout the day – especially when you've had a bad one. You deserve someone who puts as much care into you as they did when they wanted you in the beginning. Because effort shouldn't change. How much you want someone shouldn't be affected by the reality that you *have them now*.

You deserve someone who makes effort with you all the time, and not just when they've upset you because that's when they have to show you that they care. Because that's not care. That's not effort. That's realising your mistake and wanting to make it up to the other person only until the next time you mess up again.

People are quick to make excuses about why they couldn't message or call back without considering how that might make the other person feel. If you truly care about someone – you will make time for them.

There are no excuses because you don't make excuses when you want someone in your life. You don't make excuses when they're your priority. You don't make excuses when you care about them. Because if there are excuses, then there is reason to question their care. If there are excuses, then there is reason to question their concern. If there are excuses, then there is reason to question their love.

And don't let them tell you otherwise.

Protect Yourself

Sometimes, you really want it to work out. You look at the person sitting in front of you and you can't imagine being apart from them. You're scared that if they leave – it will be over for you both. The idea of letting them go seems unimaginable and unbearable.

But you need to let them go if you want to protect yourself. You need to let them go if having them in your life causes you discomfort. You need to let them go if you have more reasons for why it won't work than why it will. You need to let them go if you can't pinpoint your place in their life and if they don't make you feel good about yourself. You need to let them go if the only reason why you want to keep them close is your emotions, and nothing about whether they're good for you. Nothing about their feelings towards you, or the reality in which you find yourself in. And nothing about their behaviour towards you. Nothing about them *wanting to stay*. Because that's not real.

They need to make your life better. They should allow you to grow. Their presence in your life should be like a soft blanket, at least most of the time. They should feel like home. And, most importantly – they need to *want you too*. And if they don't – if they cause you discomfort or make you feel bad about yourself, if they're the reason for the constant uneasiness in your life, and if they aren't in it for the same reasons that you are – then they need to leave, and you need to be the one to hold the door open for them as they do.

Trust me, the moment that you start putting yourself first – you will make room for all the good that is meant to be just for you.

You are Enough

You are enough. Words that, hot on your tongue, spiral out of your mouth in urgency. Before that, they were balled up inside your throat, choking you with a rush of emotion.

You want to believe it. You want to believe that you're enough for once. That you matter. That your heart is important, and your feelings are valued. So, when those words spill out of you in a puddle of tears – your mind pleads with you to believe them. Especially after last night when, once more, your partner spilled out of the drive – and possibly out of your life – without another word. Without so much as a look back in your direction, and the life that they had with you, before setting out into a future that doesn't have you in it.

You could pour innumerable buckets of love into someone and it still won't be enough. They will still remember that one time when you didn't have them in mind or that day when you didn't put them first. They will still recall those words that rushed out of you in anger as you were up to your elbows in yet another argument. They will still point out what you did wrong and what you could have done better.

But when they leave again, their eyes planted on the blurry night ahead while you're framed by your door, arms crossed, fingers trembling, knees barely holding you upright; watching them go – remember this well – *you are enough*. These are words that should come to you as easily as the love that you hand out to others. It's not about that day when you forgot to buy them their favourite drink when you were out, or when you didn't have them in mind as you made plans. It's not about when – for the first time since you both got together – you put yourself first. It's not about the words that tumbled out of you in response to the brutal things that they said in anger. It's not about everything that you did wrong.

It's about everything that you did right.

It's about the depth of love that you showed to them. It's about all those nights out with your friends when you checked up on them and whenever you went out – on adventures, holidays or work trips – and brought them back a souvenir because you remembered them. It's about that week in January a few years ago when they were sick and you didn't leave their side, and all those occasions when you put them first – when you thought about what they needed. When you valued their opinion. When you cared about their emotions. It's about the number of times, *'I love you'*, flowed out of your mouth when you gazed deeply into their eyes, and the *'I'm sorry'*, that you croaked in urgency to be the bigger person, to step down from a fight, to put it all aside – because they mattered to you more than the point that you wanted to make.

You are enough. Especially when you empty out the contents of your heart into another person and – despite all that you do for them – they still walk away. Because you're not perfect, and if you tried your best to do everything right and all they saw was what you did wrong – then you aren't being treated fairly. And this is when you need to affirm this truth the most – that you are enough, and you always will be.

No matter who stays. My love, *you are enough.*

Love Yourself

Love yourself enough to let them go. Love yourself enough to say, 'no', when they're asking for too much. Enough to stick up for yourself. Enough to demand your right. Enough to assert it. Enough to stop giving without asking for anything in return. Love yourself enough to put yourself first. Enough to stop letting people trample all over you. Enough to say what you feel – with your head held high and your shoulders spread wide. With no fear that they might judge you, because you have nothing to shy away from.

Love yourself enough to accept your truths. Your shortcomings. Your scars. Enough to embrace your imperfections and find strength in all your vulnerabilities. Love yourself enough to wait for the love that has earned you. Enough to remove any thoughts of 'settling' on your mind. Enough to understand that the love that you need – you will receive. Enough to recognise that it hasn't worked out with anyone in the past because they weren't the right one for you. Enough to know, with certainty, that one day someone will come along and teach you how to spill self-love into all your cracks. One day someone will show you how whole you already were and how much you don't need them or anyone else to be happy. One day someone will show you how invaluable you are.

Because the right person doesn't complete you. No.

The right person makes you better.

The right person will show you how wrong you were to find missing pieces of yourself in others – because everything that you wanted could be found within you. One day someone will come along and show you how imperfectly perfect you are. They will show you how right you were to wait. To wait for honest love. Real love. Messy. Kind and often playful love. Make sure that you consider all of this when you make your decision to walk away – because you need to be sure of what's right for you.

Love yourself enough to walk away. Please, do it for you. Love yourself enough to walk away.

Heartbreak teaches you that love changes over time.

My first heartbreak, and perhaps the worst, changed my entire life. At the time it felt like everything was over, but when I look back now – I'm certain that whatever happened, happened for the best.

My heartbreak taught me a lot about love. It taught me what to expect and what not to expect. It taught me the importance of red signals and when I should pay attention to them *(the moment they light up in front of me)*. It taught me the value of self-love and when to focus on the needs of my heart. It taught me when to *say yes* and when to *say no*. It taught me about the weight associated with loving someone, as well as the responsibilities that follow.

My heartbreak taught me that love isn't a word that should flutter out of your mouth without prior thought or contemplation of the potential consequences. And how – despite our real emotions – a lot of us use this word to justify sudden feelings that overwhelm or confuse us, for which we don't have any other title. And when the responsibilities follow, we turn at our heels and scurry out the back door before the other person can claim them. It taught me that, often love isn't enough to keep a relationship going – practicality and real-life decisions are just as important, if not more.

My heartbreak taught me the most significant truth and it is this – *love changes over time.*

The reason why I say this is because I remember very clearly; the first time that I told myself that I loved this person was when *I was hurting.* I told myself that because my ache was so raw and powerful, the only explanation for this was love. I later realised that believing you truly love someone when you're aching for them is the worst way to measure your feelings. Pining for someone doesn't constitute love. When I look back now, I wonder – *did I even love this guy?* Love, in the way that I understand love now and not in the way that I understood it then, and the answer is: **no.**

The reason why I say this is as follows: we, as humans, are constantly picking up new lessons and growing through our lived experiences. Our fluctuating lives influence our perception of the world and the concepts that we form. As a result of witnessing more of the world; the meaning of many values in our lives change. What peace means to us changes. What matters to us most changes. Our dreams and hopes change. What we want from our life changes. *We change.*

And if we change then how could love possibly stay the same?

That's why when I consider my heartbreak through my widened lens and the several years between the person I was then and the person I am now – I realise that it wasn't love.

Some people view each encounter of love as being just as significant, which is fine. However, some of you may look at your experiential episodes of 'love' in those two cases to notice a disparity between the two. I'm one of those people. 21-year-old-me believed that was love for what she knew it to be, but 25-year-old-me has witnessed more of love since then and doesn't feel the same way.

The truth is, a lot of us *presume* that we have an idea of the kind of person we want to be with, but we're not certain until we come across them. It's for this reason, whenever our heart breaks – our emotions for that person are so significant that we tell ourselves *we can never love someone again*. We don't consider the possibility that there's someone better out there for us. We don't reason with our shuddering heart that there may be someone more suited to us, someone who can make us undeniably happy and truly loving us, the kind of love that is more real than anything we've ever experienced.

This doesn't mean that your heartbreak wasn't valid, or that you weren't *in love*. Because you were. You were in love with them for *what you knew to be love at that time*. This could be anything from fierce feelings that we usually associate with love to something subtle and calm. It could be what you've learnt about love in books and TV, or foetal emotions built around the *potential* of love between you two.

Yes, love is a verb. An action. It's what you do for someone else.

But the characteristics of love, the depth, warmth and impact are different for each of us and change over time. For me, love could be a deep friendship with someone who wants to grow together. For someone else love could be a joint sense of purpose. For you, love could be the adrenaline rush caused by someone's presence in your life. Perceptions of love can change within a single person as well. When I was younger, love was passing by each other in the hallways, being excited about seeing them and having a laugh. As I grew older, a progressive mindset became more important to me. And now, I'm more likely to fall for someone who not only brings me a sense of adventure but also has a progressive vision, works hard or has a purpose. Of course, being a good and honest human being is also at the top of the list now. Compared to a few years ago, my definition of love has become stable as opposed to what it was; *temperamental and at face-value.*

Imaginably when I get even older: peace, quiet and a tranquil life will appeal to me more than an active, productive one. And someone who brings this in my life will be the one that I love the most. Hopefully, this will be the same productive and adventurous person that I fall in love with today – because we will grow together.

For most people, this is the case. Their concept of love shifts over time with the same person – because they grow together. Love doesn't stay the same in their relationship – it shouldn't – and as they both go on individual and joint journeys; love moulds into what they both need in their relationship.

For those of you *(like myself)* who haven't had a long-term relationship or stayed with one partner for more than a few months – your concept of love might change after each break up. The person whom you were with before the breakup was what you needed then, but when your heart breaks – you lose a part of yourself and end up finding out new stuff about yourself that transform the meaning of love for you. The next person that you fall for might be completely different to the first, or even if they're similar – *the love that you share will be different.*

The truth is, although the first time your heart breaks and you conclude that you will never love the same way again – which is partly true – *you do fall in love again* and it's just as beautiful. Even if love the second time around, or third, is not the same as the one before that – it's still special. It's different, that's all. It is different because nothing stays the same and sometimes, we re-evaluate our beliefs and ideas about the world after things fall apart in our small one.

I know that heartbreak sucks. It's absolutely horrible. But believe me when I tell you that you learn to love again. You do. Because your heart is an ocean of love and it will always have enough to give to others. Love changes over time, which is fine. It's what we need because if love stayed the same while *we changed* then we wouldn't need love in our lives anymore.

The truth is that love changes as we get older.

You can accept this all-rounded truth and let it make you feel better about your heartbreak. Because it means that you will fall in love again and it will be magical. It means that you won't run out of love or become numb – not for long anyway. It means that the right person exists and you're closer to finding them than you think. It means that love will shape into what you need, and you won't compromise for less.

Alternatively, you can take this all-rounded truth as predictive of how your hurt will fade away over time – and allow this to make you feel better. Love as you know it will change, and once you uncover more of life – you will stop pining for them. You won't miss them. You won't see them, or your heartbreak, in the same way again. You will understand love in a new way altogether and according to that definition of love – you will no longer love them at all.

In fact, love will change so much that you might question whether you ever loved them – like I ended up doing.

This doesn't mean that your current emotions aren't valid.

It doesn't mean that you're not justified in grieving what you lost. It doesn't mean that your perception of the heartbreak is wrong, nor does it brush off your process of healing as insignificant. It only means that when you look back at your heartbreak – you will no longer be uncomfortable because of it. And when you fall in love again, you will take this heartbreak as a stepping-stone in your life that nurtured you. You will see everything that was wrong in that relationship and your concept of love will shift according to this new awareness.

Even though this heartbreak is pounding inside your chest right now, with time you will see this episode in your life as a vital step in your life that shaped you into the person that you were meant to be.

Take your time. Take as much of it as you need.

Because your heartbreak is valid, it's real and it's painful. This heartbreak is just as substantial as the one before it, and the one before that. You don't need to give any explanations for the second or third time that you experience heartbreak.

One of the negative consequences of this idea that love changes over time is that your heart will continue to break if your concept of love *doesn't transform into a positive and healthy one* and continues to be toxic/unhealthy. But a positive consequence of this is that you will forget your previous heartbreak(s) when you fall headfirst into the *'right kind of love'*.

As I said before, when I mention the *'right kind of love'* I'm not saying that this love doesn't come without its difficulties and hardships. *Because it is hard.* It will take a lot out of you and it will demand more than you thought it could. But this doesn't mean that the *'right love'* isn't honest, pure and good for you. This love is the one that makes you feel safe, secure and content. It's the one that fills your ribs with liquid warmth. It's the love that was yours all along.

All the heartbreaks before this one will disappear into the past. You won't even remember them. Because that's how beautiful the love that you deserve is going to be.

Love

Falling in love is beautiful and you should embrace it.

I find it harder to write about love (the falling, filled with a burst of excitement and passion) than about heartache. Because, in all honesty – I've fairhandedly come across the latter more than the former. In the past, I was shown more about what love is/isn't by getting my heart broken rather than by *loving* itself.

When you go through your fair share of heartache, you start associating love with all those negative concepts. You start to believe that love kills. It shatters. That love is toxic. Love is tangled up emotions. It is uncomfortable turmoil. It is tear-soaked pillows and sleepless nights. It is emptiness. It is questions rattling through your mind. It is misery. Anguish. Grief. Loss. It is not being *enough* or being *too much*.

The truth is that love isn't any of those horrible moments in our lives, and it took me a while to figure that out.

Especially when you initially fall in love. The rush of glee. The nervous jitters. The flutter of anticipation over what will happen next. The heat that rises to your face when you think of them. Your heartbeat, pattering against your unhinged chest when you're near them. The dots of red on your cheeks when they compliment you, or look at you for long, extended periods of time. The sensation of utter completeness. It's like you've been dipped into melted happiness for the longest time.

But a lump of fear forms at the pit of your stomach.

Your pulse quickens when you consider whether you've imparted more than you should have – about your past, your family, your trauma or your dreams. You don't know how much you were supposed to say, or what you should reveal as you both embark on this new adventure. You're uncertain about the level of attention that you should give them, or whether you should peel off your mask from the onset and be yourself entirely.

I'm guilty of having all those anxious thoughts. But the one lesson that I've taken from it all is this – the experience of falling in love is more enjoyable when you *stop worry too much*. When you let love take its course – the reign of both your hearts in its power – that's when you're totally free and able to appreciate the exhilaration of falling. That's when you're able to truly enjoy all the small bursts of emotions that are making an appearance in your life.

Fear holds you back. It wraps itself around your ankle and stops you from moving forward, especially when you cross an emotional pedestal with someone. Fear of getting your heart broken or falling too quickly. Fear of loving too much or too little. Fear of not being capable to love them back. Fear of giving too much of yourself away. Fear of not being strong enough to commit. Fear of making a mistake or of never being enough. Fear of them not being the one.

Fear is what stops us from loving at all.

But love is free. It's fully immersive. Love is a beautiful ride, one that you must take with your eyes open if you want to make the most of it. So, you need to get the seed of fear out of your mind and crush it under your feet – especially if fear doesn't come with a reason.

Some of the most stunning memories that you will make in your relationship will be when you're first falling for them. The level of mystery, the lack of control over your emotions and the direction they're taking you in – coupled with a slight unfamiliarity regarding this new person – builds for a magical adventure that you both embark on.

To begin with, *you will be scared*. It's only natural to be. But love is the opposite of fear. Love brings you closer to your senses. Love is the wind that allows you to fly and the gravity that grounds you. Let fear make you cautious, if you will, but don't let it stop you from falling in love.

The first phase of falling in love is the most beautiful. *Embrace it*. Welcome it with open arms. Pull the door wide open to let love in. No matter what happens and where this new journey takes you, love will transform your life forever. *It really will.*

What Love Means

I'm trying to understand love. I'm trying to absorb it in its entirety, and this is really difficult to do. Not *'loving'* itself. Not the love where you gaze into their eyes and find your glowing reflection in their dark pearls, because their heart is now with yours. Not the love where you're giddy when you're with them, or when you always hold their hand and smile when they're by your side – but the hard stuff.

The love that is imperfect, painful and jarring. The love that causes you to say unpleasant words without thinking twice about them, then churn with regret over the way that those words made your partner feel later. The love where you hold onto your beliefs, no matter how harsh they are, and refuse to back down – even when your partner tries their best to convince you. The love that is foolish and unable to see beyond your own aching. The love that is jealous, insecure, mean and inconsiderate.

But also – *the love that is afraid of losing them.*

The love that asks you to make compromises and sacrifices. The love that urges you to bite your tongue when you bubble with anger and to let it go – even when your mind doesn't agree. The love that puts its grief to the side and learns to put them first. The love that hurts as much as it heals.

Love comes in every shade. The love that makes you both happy is also the love that can hurt you both, and it is the balance between hurting and happiness that I need to find. So,

I'm still trying to understand love in its entirety. And I know that even when I'll consider that I've got it all figured out – I will uncover more about love as time goes on. I will find bright shades as I delve further into love. I will come to terms with what love is and what it isn't. I'll learn about when love is a balm to your heart and food for your soul and when it has the potential to turn you into stone.

I will keep learning and keep experiencing love, and perhaps one day – after taking adventures with the person who gives me this love – I will finally uncover what love truly means to me.

Fear of Falling

Sometimes, you're not confused about the other person – you're scared.

You're scared that even if you let your walls down, they might not. You're scared that perhaps you will let them in and show them your weaknesses and your darkness – but they won't do the same. Or maybe they won't like what they see. And after you've uncovered every part of yourself, they will look at you and no longer see the beautiful person that they thought you were. You're scared that you will let them in and, when you start to trust them, they will break your trust and crush your soul. You're scared that you might begin to love someone again, you might let your heart feel what it hasn't for so long – but they won't appreciate it.

They won't value your softness or your emotions, and in the end, they will let you go. And that's what scares you the most.

Sometimes you're not confused about whether they're the one – you're worried that they are. What if they are everything that you've been searching for, but they don't feel the same way about you? You're scared that you will jump off your lifeboat into the uncertainty of love – *and they might break your heart and walk away.*

Be with This Person

Be with the person who makes your dreams their own.

The person who wakes you up each morning before the sun does and motivates you to greet the day with a smile on your face. The person who supports you as you work hard towards all your goals. Be with the person who believes in you more than you believe in yourself. The person who waves off your concerns and tells you how much potential you have, not because you need to hear it from them but because *you need to hear it*. Be with the person who looks at you with a warmth in their eyes that melts love between your bones. The person who loves you fiercely and in every single way.

Be with the person who is always there for you.

The person who will look out for you when you're down, when you need them, when it's your big day and when nothing's going right. Be with the person who loved you yesterday, loves you today and will continue to love you tomorrow. The person who knows what it means to love someone. The person who recognises that love isn't just an emotion, it's an action. It's a promise. Love is what you do for someone else. It is being there. It is showing up. It is prioritising.

Be with the person who appreciates the responsibilities that come with loving someone. The person whose smile is enough to tell you how much you mean to them and how – no matter what happens – their love for you will never fade. Be with this person, *and with this person only*.

Dear Self

The right person is good for you.

There are many insights that I've had about love over the last few years, and perhaps the most important one is this – *the right person is good for you.* But what do I mean when I say, *'good for you'?*

Simply put – they're not bad for you. They don't intentionally cause you grief. They don't put their ego before your relationship. They want the best for you. Their actions fall in accordance with their words. They put you first. They cherish you. They respect you. They don't purposely make you feel bad about what you say or do. They're not condescending. They value your goals and dreams. And most importantly – *they value you.*

The right person is good for you because being with them brings abundance in every aspect of your life. This doesn't mean that they won't make those mistakes at least once in your relationship out of ignorance. But the *potential for improvement* in your relationship is there – which is so important.

How many of you have been in relationships where you slowly declined?

A relationship where, even if things started off well, they got worse as time went on. Perhaps the situation was always bad, and you didn't figure it out until it hit you in the face later.

Take a look at all the different scenarios where relationships like this exist. Perhaps you were with someone who *always* needed your help, so you pushed everything else in your life away. Your partner was struggling, and you prioritised their wellbeing over yours for the first few days, then weeks, followed by months and years until you forgot what it was like to think about yourself at all. Maybe your partner didn't care about your future aspirations to begin with and they demanded that you spend all your time with them.

Or perhaps you were in a relationship where being with them consumed you wholly because you thought that you found the *sole reason* for your joy, so you couldn't think about anything else. No, you *didn't want to* think about anything else. You forgot about your friends and your family. You no longer cared about your job, or your dreams and aspirations. Or you did care. You cared about it all; your family and friends and your studies, your job and your dreams. But your partner made you feel guilty about it, so you tried hard not to care. You tried hard to prove this to them. You tried hard not to work hard. Not to study hard, not to pour attention into yourself and, instead, give every ounce of love and care that you had to them.

Maybe your relationship was a different one where your partner didn't make any of those demands, but their behaviour *clearly showed you* that they wanted it. Or they did tell you – they demanded that you give them your everything. They glared at you with eyes that were hot with needy frustration as they served you an ultimatum – it was them or your dreams. It was them or your loved ones. It was them or your peace of mind. It was them or you.

You lost yourself in the process.

You had no idea who you were becoming. You forgot who you were without them. And after each argument – as they pushed you away – their actions forced you to hang on to them even more. You couldn't imagine being away from them. The thought of *not being with them* suffocated you. But you never realised that *being with them* was what was truly suffocating you. Your dreams went out of the window. So did your hopes for the future. Frankly, *there was no future* if they weren't with you. As a result, you gave them your everything. Their dreams became your dreams, and the only thing that mattered was keeping them happy.

We've all encountered at least one version of the above scenarios, and in all those variations the truth is evident – *you were with the wrong person.* Because the right person doesn't take over your life in such a manner that you forget to eat, sleep, drink or enjoy yourself. The right person doesn't overwhelm you to the point where your whole existence revolves around them, and them only.

But let me clarify first that this is different to when you first get to know someone. Those early weeks/months are incredibly consuming. You think about them all the time. You replay conversations in your mind. You make time to see them as much as you can, and a lot of your other priorities momentarily take a backseat – which is fine.

That initial *'getting to know'* period is perhaps the most engrossing in your whole relationship. It's a new connection and you're not sure where it's headed. As a result, you invest more time and as much of your energy as you can into it. You put more thought into what you do and say because it's unknown territory. You're consumed and/or intrigued by the mystery of where this relationship is headed. But after a while, when everything settles down and you've found the person that you want to be with – they are *an addition* to your happy life. They don't become the sole reason for it.

The right person doesn't devour your life in the way that the wrong person does.

They don't guilt-trip you when you put your needs first. In fact, they push you to make decisions that prioritise your wellbeing, because the right person knows how unfair you've been with yourself in the past. The right person realises that you've given more to others than you've received. This is why they want you to expend your energy on your own needs without putting any pressure on you to give large chunks of your time to them. The right person gives you as much as they can without asking the same of you in return – at least not until you want to and are ready for it.

The right person is aware that your heart has been ribbed with pain on more occasions than you can remember. They're aware that you carry your heart on your sleeve and will always have enough to give to others – so, they don't expect you to rip your heart out and hand it to them. They want to earn your heart, and your love – and when they do, they will do whatever they can to keep it safe.

The right person doesn't just cause a rush of nervousness in your heart but also produces the calm waves in your mind. Their presence brings you peace in a way that no one else's presence ever has before. You no longer feel like you're in a race, instead – life finally becomes the steady journey that you always had faith it would be.

The right person doesn't pull you away from your dreams or aspirations. In fact, they urge you to work hard, to put your time and effort into your career and to become the best version of yourself.

The right person wants you to spend time with those that you love – your family, your friends, the people that cheer you up and make you smile. The right person doesn't overwhelm your life in a way that it becomes hard for you to focus on anything else. And if they do, then they overwhelm you in the right way. They overwhelm your heart with love, support and friendship. They overwhelm your peace of mind by becoming the reason why your eyes often crinkle with smiles. They overwhelm your happiness by making you laugh so much that your cheeks ache, the kind of happiness that doesn't leave you even when they're not physically present. They overwhelm your strength by standing by you, their fingers stringed through yours as you face all your battles.

Remember when you were in love before. How their eyes were lined with self-efficacy and they had the ability to instantly fill you with guilt? Remember whenever you tried to do something for yourself and they brushed it away without a second thought.

Your wishes weren't important. Your dreams weren't important. What you wanted wasn't more important than them. And no matter how hard you tried, you always felt like you would never be enough. Remember when you thought that this was all that love could give you. You thought that love could only bring you to your knees in agony but not gift you the joy that you expected. Love couldn't cherish you. Love couldn't take care of you. Love couldn't raise you off the ground so your wings could soar you to the sky. Love couldn't do more than feel like a knife twisting inside your chest.

Then you meet the right person and all your negative beliefs fly out the window. Your fears about love. Your past experiences. Your memories of love turning your heart cold. Of love making you question yourself. Of love breaking you. Love leaving you. Love never turning back. All you know about love now is that it's good. It is safe. It is kind. All you picture of love now is bright blue skies cross-stitched with flocks of birds and a sun that hangs above like a huge yellow pendant. All you believe about love now is that it heals, it's magical and it brings with it a hurricane of contentment. But this only happens when you're with the right person and not the wrong.

Remember, the right person exists and they're everything that you ever wanted and more.

With the wrong person, love is a red, gruesome battlefield that you're destined to lose. With the right person, love is a diving adventure. It's a wonderful ride. With the right person, love is the balm to all your aches. With the right person, love heals rather than breaks. With the right person, love can become your strength and not your weakness. With the right person, love becomes the actuality of a magnificent dream that you've always dreamt.

With the right person – love can give you the strength that you need to save yourself. It really can.

And believe me, *it does.*

Ocean-like Heart

Have you ever questioned someone's love for you?

Where, a trail of broken promises and heartbreak have led you to conclude that you're not worthy of love – so, why would this person love you? How could they possibly love you when those before them didn't? What do they see? Why do they feel this strongly about you? Because when you look in the mirror – you only see brokenness. When you look at your reflection, you see someone who was given love in small rubbles and pity pieces. You see someone who wanted to keep warm, but love was just a thin coat that barely covered a fraction of your heart – but you still made do.

Then this person comes along. This wonderful, gentle beam of sunshine that lights up your life with a love that's plentiful. With a love that's certain that you can pour into your own cracks and it will be there to build alongside you. With a love that doesn't say *no*. With a love that puts you first, that strips off all questions and ambiguities and means it when it says, '*I love you*'.

But your mind feels like a washing machine, rumbling hard and fast with fear that maybe this is too good to be true. Maybe you're temporary for them and when they find someone better, they'll scurry along and leave you in fragments all over again. Maybe you're dreaming and once you wake up from this silky image, cradling you in your sleep; reality will hit you like a hard, cold slap in the face again.

But your fears aren't real.

You need to trust the love that you receive and know that this person sees everything in you that others did too, but they were too afraid of your magic. They were scared that they wouldn't be able to give you the depth of love that you could give them, and that's why they left. That's why they never stayed. That's why they took the easy route out rather than witnessing the magic of your soul unfold before them. Believe me when I say that the person who loves you now is sure of your courageous nature. They're certain of your magnificence. They celebrate your strength and are in awe of your vast, deep, ocean-like heart.

And this person, this human who can answer all your questions regarding what they see in you – they would happily drown in that ocean if you let them.

Thank You

Thank you for coming into my life.

Thank you for changing the direction of my existence towards something better. You've allowed me to bloom in so many ways that I don't know what I was doing before. I thought that I had it all figured out. I thought that I knew exactly where I was going and that the flow of my current life was at its best. But you came along, and it all became crystal clear. I realised then that I could become a better version of myself. I saw both my imperfections and perfections and understood what it means to let growth in, what it means to let experiences impart useful knowledge and what it means to let love in. I started valuing my dreams more and became determined in ways I never imagined. I became more whole by myself than I've ever been before.

And I know that it's down to me – the hard work, the hours that I put in, the way that I treat people. And the value that I give myself.

But still, I thank you because you pushed me to test my limits. I thank you because you want to see me reach the same heights that I see for myself. I thank you because you're compassionate, funny and selfless. Because you're my best friend. Because I had no idea how much impact another person could have on my life until I met you. I thank you because you really are something special.

I thank you – because I love you and I am so grateful for you.

Loving Someone

We believe that all our questions get answered when we find *the one.*

You tell yourself that it would be easy. You think that once you're with the love of your life, everything will sail smoothly, and the worst of your difficulties will be behind you. But truth is – loving someone doesn't come without its fair share of struggles. It's not that simple. Because with loving someone comes immense responsibility and emotional commitment.

It's not just about getting dressed and going out on dates, sending cute *'couple'* memes to each other, or texting each other and spending hours on the phone. It's not about posting photos on Instagram with #couplegoals or showing each other off whenever you can.

When you love someone, you are accountable to keep them as happy as you can, and you give them the responsibility to keep you happy. When you love someone, you put all your trust into them and expect them not to break it. When you love someone, you include them in your plans, your daily routine, your adventures and your expectations for the future. When you love someone, you peel off your walls and show them your vulnerabilities. When you love someone, you give them a huge chunk of your heart, if not all, and pray that they will be gentle towards it. When you love someone, they become the key to a lot of your joy – but a lot of your discomfort too.

Sure, they're not the sole reason for you feeling whole. But they balance you in a way that makes you *feel complete*. They bring you so much peace that if they weren't there, you would feel their absence like a hole the size of a brick in your heart.

When you love someone, you're not ignorant of the possibility that there may come a time when they're not in your life and you will have to learn how to live without them. But you take strength from this rather than let it become your weakness. When you love someone, you walk together rather than alone. When you love someone – you become a team.

Love and relationships aren't easy. But when you love someone, nothing else matters, because at the end of it – loving them is so damn worth it.

I Love You

I love you.

I love the way that you smile. Your whole face lights up, especially your eyes as they twinkle and squint, causing delicate thin lines to shoot out from the corners of your lids. I love your laughter. A deep, infectious chuckle, sending jolts of warmth through me as I join in with you – wishing fiercely that this moment never ends. I love your heart. As hard as it looks on the outside, it's as soft and squishy on the inside. And when that heart propels you to do something for me, to be there, to listen, understand and apologise – even when it's not your fault – I realise how vast it is. I grasp then that you have more room than I ever will inside that heart for others.

I love you.

When you pick on me and laugh at your own jokes and I can't help but giggle too because *it was a good one.* When you pull me up on what I did wrong. When you're honest about truths that I refuse to admit. When you wish me well and cheer me on. When you have confidence in my dreams and push me towards them. When you appreciate me and my soft, pulsing heart. When you treat me with care and compassion. And when you're there for me, even though you're equally as hurt.

I love you.

Even when I didn't realise it. Even when we barely knew each other. And when we first became friends. When we went on our first date. When you said a few lines on the phone in that coarse voice of yours and something trickled through my mind, but I couldn't decipher what it was. When you held my hand for the first time and when we hugged. I loved you when we were talking in that tiny room at your workplace and you got up to stretch and accidentally knocked out my head with your elbow, and we laughed for ages. I hadn't laughed like that in a while. It's one of my favourite memories of us.

I knew it then. The thought that had come to me a few weeks earlier and it echoed in my mind right then in that small office space.

'I love you', it said.

I love you.

Even when you didn't say it, and when you refused to admit it. When you hugged me tight and the words were on your lips but didn't leave your mouth – I still loved you. And when you finally uttered those words on that magical wintry night in London as the lights twinkled around us and the stars shone in the sky. And I will continue loving you. I will love your heart and I will love your smile. I will love your eyes. I will love your hands and I will love your hugs. I will love your soul. I will love your energy. I will love your strength and your kindness. I will always love you. Just like I do now. Just like I did then. Just like I do every time I hear you speak, smile, or laugh in that adorable way.

I love you more today than I ever did before, and less than I will love you tomorrow.

Choose this Person

Choose the person who appreciates you. Choose the person who cherishes every fragment, curve and edge of your existence. The person who accepts your shortcomings wholeheartedly and doesn't want to change a thing. The person who makes time for you. The person who gives you a call to hear your voice and make sure that you eat on time. The person who reminds you to put yourself first. Choose the person who wants you. The person who looks at you as though they've found everything that they were looking for. The person whose one gaze devours you completely.

Choose the person who is your best friend. The person who listens to all your worries, the person whom you can't hide anything from, no matter how hard you try. The person who is a part of you, an extension, another limb that keeps you going. Choose the person who brings peace to your soul.

Choose the person who loves you.

The persons who cares for you unconditionally. The person who will never let go of your hand – no matter how difficult it gets. Choose the person your heart chooses. The person whom, every time you see them, it feels like you're seeing them for the first time. The person who makes you laugh, cry and feel giddy with joy that they exist, because a world without them would be a lonely place. Choose the person who's your home. The person with whom spending hours is as easy as breathing. The person who brings out the best in you.

Choose the person who only needs to sit beside you and hold your hand tight as you both look ahead – and suddenly the future becomes a bright, beautiful place that you can't wait to grow towards together.

Some people can change your life for the better.

I'm an advocate for being self-sufficient. For relying on yourself and not depending on others for your growth. But this doesn't mean that good people can't bring about positivity in your life. It doesn't mean that others don't have the ability to impact your life in a tremendous way. Because the truth is that the right people can make your life better in countless ways.

All my writing comes from experience.

And my experiences have taught me that when you fall in love with the right person – your life changes for the better. We see it on TV and read about it in books. We watch intently as it unreels in music videos and our favourite movies, secretly wishing that we can witness this too. Then we observe our friends in toxic relationships and witness our favourite celebrity couples break up after years and children together.

We watch our parents break up and rush through a few heartbreaks ourselves. And as we get older, reality hits us that none of those movies, books and TV shows were real to begin with. As a result, we act like we don't believe in *true love*. We start to tell ourselves that it's all bogus and we're practical individuals who only focus on working hard rather than living in a dreamland. But deep down – we want to fall in love too.

It's for this reason that when you speak to someone new, a flame of hope lights up inside you.

That tiny inkling indicating that perhaps you will get your *'happily ever after'*. But time ticks on and it turns out that they weren't the one. Neither was the one after them, or the one after that. The flicker of light, indicating that you might find true love, slowly dwindles until it fades away completely. You start to believe once more that it's all an illusion. Love can't be magical, good or healthy. Movies are lying. Songs are lying. Books are lying. *People are lying*. Because the only relationships that you've observed are the ones where there are slammed doors, spiteful words and damp pillows. The only couples you've witnessed are the ones that swear, scream and shout. The only love that you've experienced is the one that makes false promises before it leaves.

Love doesn't stay. People don't stay. So, why should you trust them?

Why would you – in your right mind – fall in love when a part of you knows that they will leave, just like the others? You throw away your romance novels. You stop watching movies that portray false ideas of togetherness and forever. You switch off the radio when your favourite love song comes on. Because there are no happy or a long-lasting-relationships. There are no happily-ever-afters.

But there is. Not so much a *'happily ever after'* as there is a *'we are still evolving, learning and working on it-ever after'*. Yes, I know that this version is much more complicated and sounds more demanding – but it's the one that's real.

The truth is that you don't need someone who will give you happiness forever – without any arguments, challenges or rough patches (for one thing, that's not real). You need someone that will stay. You need someone who will look you in the eye and say, *'I want to make it work'*, and won't let go of your hand even when the path gets rocky. You need a partner who will be committed to you and whose words *'I'll always be here'* will be followed by actions that respect your relationship.

I was negative towards love for much of my life. All my encounters shaped my perception of love. I believed that love was horrible. I didn't need it in my life. Love made you weak. It made you reliant on someone else. It pushed you to forget your dreams. To ignore your purpose. To deny yourself of self-care and affection. To neglect your heart and soul. I told myself that others could only make your life worse, not better. And love made you selfish and weak.

I now realise how wrong I was.

Because the only truth that I live by these days is this – the right person will transform your life for the better.

If you're in a relationship and you notice your life diminishing at every bend – then they're not the right person for you. When you're in relationship and you notice improvements in your life; there are changes that your partner has directly contributed to or that have worked out as a result of them being in your life – *then you're with the right person*.

The truth is that some people come into your life and change it for the better. They don't bring tools or a plan through which they're going to *'fix you'* – remember, *no one else can fix you* – or solve all your problems. Instead, they bring perspective. They bring a new way of viewing the world which slowly affects you and widens your lens. Sometimes they actively try to enhance the overall quality of your life through positive actions and problem-solving, making you thankful that you have them. But most of the time, they don't need to do much in order for there to be a positive shift in your life. It happens naturally.

Improvements in your personal and professional life, in your appearance, energy, mood and your relationships are an inevitable consequence of the right person's existence. Sometimes their presence is all you need to motivate you to get up in the morning. Having them by your side gives you the courage to make effort in your dwindling relationships. Knowing that they are there, and you can turn to them whenever you need to, instantly uplifts you. You change for the better. You glow more. Smile more. Laugh more. You work harder. You make more time for those that you love. You say kinder words. You're gentler. You're more open to adventures, or perhaps you're not anymore and you turn inwards, but the point is – the improvements in your life are *what you always needed*.

This doesn't mean that your partner is *the only person* who can enhance your life. Remember, if there's anyone who can do that without the support of others – it's you. But what you need to learn is that if you're in a healthy relationship, these are the positive changes that you should notice in your life. That's all. And if you see yourself declining, then they're not the right person for you.

Some people come into your life and you had no idea that they had the key to the door that led to your peace. But that's the thing, they have the key and *they give it you* – but only you know which door to use it on. Only you know how the key works. Only you know what will truly make you happy. These people can furnish you with a new perspective, with energy and with love, but it's up to you to grab those openheartedly. It's up to you to use your fresh perspective to make a healthy change in your life. It is only up to you.

Some people come into your life and transform it forever, but it is up to you to have the strength to let them in. It is up to you to embrace them, and love, into your life for as long as it stays. It's up to you to take the key and open the door to let light in.

It's up to you to let only those who are good for you, *stay with you*.

What Love is

Love is the absence of ego. It's the absence of selfishness. It's the absence of acting for your own benefit without any regard for how it would affect the other person. It's the absence of hatred, the one that spills in where love was supposed to, eliminating all room for a warm feeling that would make your life better. Love is the absence of darkness. It's the beginning of a light that shines into your world and makes it brighter. It's the absence of greed, where you want more for yourself rather than those around you. Because love gives without asking for anything in return. It doesn't demand favours, or actions, or stuff in exchange for all that it delivers to others.

Love is the absence of power. Power that engulfs you. Power that demands that you control them and whatever goes on in their life. The kind of power that plays mind games and treats them so badly that they're left with tears trickling down their cheeks for weeks at night. Love doesn't boast power over their life, instead, *it gives the one that you love* power so that they're strong and in control of their life.

Love is the absence of acquisition. Loving someone doesn't mean that you need them for yourself, especially if they don't love you back. Loving someone means wanting the best for them, even if the best isn't with you. Loving someone means accepting that perhaps their happiness lies somewhere else, and not with you. Loving someone means allowing this truth to settle inside your tumbling heart and letting them go – *even if it hurts you.* Love doesn't mean to gain. Yes, spending the rest of your life with the person that you love would be a dream come true. But not all dreams are meant to be fulfilled and not all lovers are supposed to remain together.

And when you accept this, no matter how much it tugs at your heartstrings and breaks you – that's when you will be certain that you truly loved them. Because you loved them enough to let them go.

When You Love Someone

When you love someone there is the undeniable fear of losing them. The thought of not having them by your side hangs heavy like a grey cloud above your head every day, every moment as your heart pushes further into the unfamiliarity of love. The possibility of them waking up one morning and no longer wanting you, or that events may unfold which will result in you two parting ways causes a knot of pain between your ribs. Actual pain, like a burning tornado inside your heart every time you feel it.

When you love someone there is vulnerability, trust and giving away pieces of your soul to your partner. When you love someone there is the dread that losing them will break your heart, and if they were to leave your side, a huge part of you will leave too.

It's hard, loving someone. Confiding in them. Looking at them for the answers to all the questions that you've been searching for and, even if they don't have the answers, even if they're trying to figure life out in the way that you are – knowing that with them by your side life will be easier somehow, adds to the anxiety of losing them. It adds to the hurt that will follow.

But when you love someone there is easy laughter that seeps into your bones. When you love someone there are adventures, a warmth inside your chest and interactions that you will remember for lifetimes to come. When you love someone there's the tiny voice in your head that says, *'Finally, there you are'*, when you see them. There is peace that you never knew that you could find – but you do. *You do.* When you love someone there's a friendship that will never leave you feeling cold. When you love someone there are new adventures, breakfasts in bed, early morning walks and late nights spent under the stars which – no matter how far you go – you will never forget.

When you love someone there is fear, sure, but there's also a fearlessness that you didn't know you could summon. When you love someone there is peace of mind – peace that pours from your heart to the rest of you. Peace that you embrace with open arms. Peace that stays.

Believe me – it is peace that stays.

The One You Deserve

The one you deserve will know what to do with all of you, and not just the parts that they like. They won't judge you for your past regrets. They will be honest with you. They will pull you up when you make mistakes and they will support you as you correct them. They will hold your hand tight as you grasp all the crucial lessons that life hands you down. They will let you heal in your time. They will appreciate your rough edges without aiming to *'perfect'* you. They will cherish the heart between your ribs, soft and bubbling with relentless love – and they will do their best to tend to it.

The one you deserve will try to protect you as much as they can, but they'll know that most of the battles in your life are ones that you need to fight alone. The one you deserve will give you your space when you need it, as well as welcome you into theirs. They won't push you away, or make you feel guilty for being with yourself for a while. They will urge you to make time for yourself. They will encourage you to grow, change and become comfortable under your skin. The one you deserve will appreciate all of you, and not just the outer layers – filled with light-hearted moments, banter and sunlight. But the darkness too. And the muggy parts. The jagged pieces. The anguish. The trauma. The emotions that you can't voice. All of it.

The one you deserve will love every ounce of you – showing you that love isn't something that you have to earn, *it never was to begin with.*

Love Hurts

It's not that love doesn't hurt. Of course, it hurts. Even when you love a kind-hearted person. Even when you're in a healthy relationship. Even when both you and your partner put each other first, try to do everything right and show each other love, care and affection. Even when you want the best for each other. Even when there are days when happy tears are streaming down your face, and your arms are wrapped around your stomach because it hurts from laughing so much. *Even then.*

Love hurts and it's a fact of life.

Think of it this way – you are two different people. With varying upbringings. With worldviews that have moulded along with the people you became. Of course, you're going to have disagreements. You will want one thing and they will want another. Sometimes their behaviour might hurt you and your behaviour might hurt them. Because what's right/wrong for you both will vary. But that doesn't mean that this relationship isn't right for you. It doesn't mean that they're not right for you.

The truth is that there's a huge difference between *toxic love* and *love that is good for you.* Sure, both will have varying levels of arguments, disagreements and moments of unclarity/confusion about why you're having problems. But the difference is this; when love is healthy – the disagreements don't matter. They're a mere blip in the big, beautiful picture of your relationship. When love is good for you – you work through it. You meet halfway. You don't purposely hurt the other person. You don't put your ego first. You don't put your priorities first, at least not at the cost of their welfare. You adjust to become better versions of yourselves together. You work on the relationship as a team. You don't give up on each other. You use your arguments to build your relationship and make it stronger.

Love does hurt. It's a fact of life.

But the difference is that the wrong relationship takes you down and rips your love apart with every argument, disagreement and inconvenience.

But the right relationship – it always brings you both together.

One day, you will find the right person. Until then – be the right person for yourself.

All I've advocated for in my previous books is healing and moving on by yourself – which is very important. Being self-reliant and depending on yourself when you're rebuilding your life is essential. But it's not the only way to go about it, and I don't want you to think that I'm crossing out the possibility of having invaluable relationships with people who bring you peace as your heart mends itself. Because the truth is that friendships build you. Family grounds you. And love – love gives you wings that allow you to fly.

I want you to hold on to this truth: "One day you will find the right person and they will be everything that you wanted and more, but until then – you need to be the right person for yourself."

You can create this image of someone that you want to spend the rest of your life with, but you don't know who that will be until they're in front of you. Meanwhile, you can construct an idea of what they might be like – but they are the ones who will fill in the colours and turn your idea into a reality, *which is so exciting.*

Love is beautiful and it's great to look forward to falling into it. But I don't want you to let the expectation of falling in love consume you. Because the truth is that until love comes along – when it comes along, and *if it comes along* – you need to be the right person for yourself.

A lot of us are lucky to find someone to call our partner and stay with them, but some of us only get that opportunity for a short while. And others, others might not find what they're looking for at all. It's all part of a bigger plan, one that we don't understand until years down the line.

But you can't let this truth prickle in your heart.

Because whether you find the right person or not – you can still be the right person for yourself. You can give yourself the love, care and effort that you expect from *'the one'*. You can pick yourself up whenever you stumble and fall. You can hold your own hand as you face the next challenge in your life. You can spill love into the cracks inside your heart. You can be there for yourself in every way that your partner can.

Because we have to be our own lovers, our own *everything* before we can let someone else in.

You need to learn to be a whole person before you let another whole person in. Because love works best that way. It's the only way that love can be healthy – when it's between two equally whole people who furnish each other's growth, goals and future. And in order for you to be this whole person who enhances a relationship – *you need to be the right person for yourself.*

Focus on your goals and dreams. Sit your exams. Go to your lectures and classes. Apply to jobs that you really want. Take up new qualifications. Go out with your friends. Spend time with your family. Go travelling. Live by yourself or move in with others. Do whatever you might not when your partner is around, as well as whatever you would. Because the truth is, the right person is already by your side – *it's you.*

Take care of yourself until it's time to pass on a little bit of that responsibility to someone else. Cherish your heart, protect it and love it until you decide that it's time to share it with someone else. Until the right person comes along – *if they come along* – do whatever you need to in order to achieve a beautifully rich and abundant life. And when they finally make an entrance into your life, they will find a complete person, *a whole you,* someone who is so comfortable with themselves that they will crave to get a piece of you – just so they can taste an ounce of the brilliance that you have created for yourself.

One day, the right person will come into your life, but until then – *be the right person,* the one that you deserve to spend the rest of your life with.

Dear Self

Healing & Wellbeing

Healing is a journey. A long, fluctuating and life-altering one.

Most of my pieces are about healing. Nearly all the content that I share online is about moving forward. As well as acceptance. Change. Growth. And self-love. I talk a lot about the role that all these mini journeys play in our bigger healing journey. But I don't focus solely on moving on from heartache.

Because we heal from various experiences in our lives. We heal from forgotten friendships and difficult childhoods. We heal from broken homes and loneliness. We heal from separation, loss and many of our firsts; the first time we failed. The first time we got hurt. The first time our heart broke. The first time we couldn't complete a task or get the grade that we wanted. The first time we experienced the death of a loved one. The first time we got into a relationship.

We heal from our defeats, our unfulfilled dreams and our

declining expectations. We heal from the first heartbreak and the last. We heal from the words our mother said when we were 5 and from the all-too-real memory of our father not having time to take care of us because he was working too hard. We heal from the arguments that we had with our siblings and friends, and all the quarrels that we've had with our partner(s). We heal from every conflict that we've witnessed, as well as all the wars that we've been at the centre of.

Look at it this way – when you heal, a part of you is mending itself so that event can sit inside your mind without causing you pain. Another part of you is developing tools on how to prevent it from re-occurring or how to deal with it if it does happen again.

Healing is as complicated as it is simple.

It is as muggy as it is pure. There's no clear route. There's no accessible boulevard to pad through, with overarching skies and a glowing sun, leading the way to the finish line. There are only twisted paths, lined with trees of pain and past lessons where you dip and dive out of the way as the twines of life attempt to overpower you.

For me, healing isn't a specific destination or somewhere that I need to race to. It's not like I'll wake up one day and say, *'Aah, I've finally healed'*, and become an unscathed person once more. A blackboard with no chalk marks. A white slate. As though I haven't been jarred and weathered by experiences that took me years to get over. Healing doesn't work like that.

Healing is a journey.

One that you must take if you want to move forward.

The truth is that you will probably be more complex as a person the further you dive into your healing than you were at the beginning – but that's not a bad thing. Because the purpose of healing isn't for it to do a spring clean of all your past trauma and transform you into the person you were before you went through that awful chapter in your life. Because if that's what healing was going to do then the good chapters would vanish into thin air along with the bad. Chapters filled with knowledge that builds you and regrets that transform you. Chapters filled with fond memories and laughter. Filled with tears that cleanse you, as well as the friends that you make along the way – the ones capable of causing a revolution within you. Friends that you lose in order to regain yourself, and those that only arrived as a moral in your life and nothing more.

Chapters filled with adventures. Chapters filled with all the seeds of emotions swelling inside your heart, as well as the bead of thoughts that plant a new perspective in you.

If healing was to wash you inside out like a car and return you, sparkling clean, you would lose all the invaluable tools that you've brought with you. The ones that make you, *you*. As well as the scars that are evidence of your growth. If healing's job was to wipe your past away and transform you into someone brand new – you would lose an essential part of yourself; *your core*. You wouldn't just be cleansed of the cutting memories but also so many of the radiant ones; the ones that you turn to in your lowest times, the memories that cause the harsh corners of your mouth to lift into a soft smile, the memories that allow nostalgic tears to bundle up in your throat.

It's for this reason that healing isn't something that you wake up to one day. It's not a cure. It's not a clear-out of all your worst experiences – although it can involve a process of that sort.

Healing is a voyage through your deepest fears.

It's a long, cobbled path, lined with teachings and hardships. Healing doesn't allow you to escape your problems, but to face them. To come to terms with them. To embrace them and learn how to overcome them. It's for this reason that healing is chaotic. It takes time. It's for this reason that healing is an expedition. Because you're moving forward with the weight of all the adversities that you've experienced, aware that you won't be able to throw them out, and you're building a new you at the same time – one that encompasses all your wounds, as well as the insight – and accepting a new mindset.

It's going to take time. It's going to get grubby as you inspect, bit by bit, all the good and bad parts of your life – the love, the hurt, the anguish inside you – in order to figure out how to move forward. It's going to be a longwinded adventure of its own. It won't happen overnight. You probably won't even realise what's happening. You will go about your life, witnessing new events, meeting different people, diving into delightful new adventures while your mind connects the dots together. And it's during this time that your heart will join itself together again, piece by piece.

Healing never truly ends.

Sure, you will get to a place one day where that sequence of events – raw and tender in the beginning – will no longer bother you. Perhaps a few years down the line, it will be nothing other than a slither of recollection. But that incident will always remain a turning point for you, symbolic of a time in your life that transformed you completely and made you the person that you are today. In the beginning, that image will feel like a lump rammed inside your throat. It might cause your eyes to tear up because of everything that you went through, evidence of your strength over time. But the more time that passes, the memory will turn into a nostalgic smile – evidence of how little it will end up affecting you.

Nevertheless, that struggle will always be a part of you. It will always walk with you on your healing journey. Even if you're completely over it. Even if you no longer remember any of those people/events. Even if you've travelled across cities and have leaped into new relationships of friend, partner or parent. Even if that incident is years and years behind you – it will always be a part of you.

Not all healing journeys have the same level of impact. Not all healing journeys shape us as greatly some can – because not every ache is the same. Some healing journeys are shorter, less hurtful and not as significant, but they still contribute particles of growth to your life – this is what matters the most.

It's for this reason that healing doesn't happen overnight. And it doesn't end either, because healing is a course that involves growth and *you never stop growing*. Healing isn't going to stop, and healing isn't going to turn you into a clean slate. But healing is going to change you in ways you never imagined –

that's what you need to focus on. When you view healing in this way, it lightens the burden on your shoulders. You no longer see healing as a race that you need to finish as quickly as you can. Nor do you see it as a competition against others who appear to be closer to the finish line because they look like they're having a better time than you are.

Remember this – *appearances lie.*

The truth is – most of us are struggling to find our way back to ourselves or discover a new trajectory to a different self. Even if other people look like they're having a better time – laughing, adventuring and loving along the way – it doesn't mean that they're still not on their healing journeys. It doesn't mean that some days aren't harder than the others. It doesn't mean that they still haven't received all the answers to their questions. It doesn't mean that they don't wake up some mornings with the hangover of old hurt still pounding in their head.

When it comes to healing, or any of your life battles – *other people are not your measuring tool.* Your own progress is. Your insight is. Your previous hurting is. Your smile and moments of clarity are. Your yesteryears are. Who you were when you were drowning in discomfort, compared to the person that you now see in the mirror is. And the moment you see healing as a journey, you grasp that taking the journey is what is important, not the end goal. You understand that it's a journey that you need to take slowly rather than rushing through it. When you accept that there's no end point and you won't get a eureka moment, just moments of clarity in your life as you pulse through, you start to squeeze healing wholeheartedly against your chest. That's when you truly understand what healing can do.

Healing will nurture you.

Healing will iron out the creases of your ache. Healing will stop the heavy thrashing inside your heart. Healing will melt you back into softness. It will let you churn with emotions for as long as you want because – in the end – it will use them all to build you. It will let the tears bubble out of you – big fat meaty droplets dwindling down your cheeks. Healing will let the hurt bathe you. It will make you courageous. Healing will bring you more happiness than you ever thought possible.

Healing will also make you uncomfortable.

Healing will feel like bricks of pain have been shoved between your lungs because every time you breathe – it hurts. It will bang your heart against your ribs, as though it is trapped inside your body. It will tumble out of you as questions fluttering into thin air. Healing will tire your bones, and feel like a disoriented, difficult ride that you want to get off. It will line your eyes with burning red tears that refuse to spill down your cheeks and – sometimes – it will be the tears that gush out unapologetically anyway. Healing will be jarring. It will be hard. Heck, it will be the hardest challenge that you've ever faced.

But healing is necessary. It's an essential journey that you need to take to move on from yesterday. It's what you must do if you want to transform your life for the better, and if you want to stop hugging dark grief at night and hold onto sleep instead. And if you want to tell the monsters inside your head to leave you for good, or at least enough for you to live a normal happy life.

Healing is a magnificent, rocky ride that will transform your life forever – *and I can't wait for you to take it.*

I Will Be Okay

I want to say that I'll be okay.

I want to say it with the kind of confidence that laces my voice when I tell my friends that they will make it, and when I smile and declare that a bright beam of sunlight will shine on their face one morning and they'll feel it bursting inside their rib cage. I want to believe it for myself too. I wish that I could. I wish that the words I use to comfort others worked on me too. But it's ironic, isn't it? We're so gentle when we're dealing with our friends, family, and our lovers. We are kind to their hearts and speak with a delicateness in our tone to show them that we care, but somehow, we fail to show ourselves the same generosity – somehow, we forget that we're owed the same level of effort from ourselves.

That's where it goes wrong. Because I want to be there for myself, but my love bucket is empty when it comes to me. The hope that I have for everyone else doesn't light up inside me the moment that I consider what's right for me. But I don't blame myself for it, because this is the way we've been taught to love ourselves – in fragments. We've been shown by the world that beauty is in perfection rather than in vulnerability. We've been reminded, time and time again that sometimes you go through horrible things because you deserve it – *but I refuse* to follow this misconception any longer. I refuse to believe that I've somehow earned the kind of sorrow that I wouldn't wish upon anyone else.

It's a learning curve, one that I'll get through eventually. But for now I will be grateful for the love that I give myself, even if it's in rubbles. I want to say that I'll be okay and, one day, have faith in this to my core. But for now, I will hold my heart in my palms and be tender with it. And kind. For now, I will hold my heart and be patient for that one morning when a bright beam of daylight finally shines on my face too.

For now, I will have faith that I will get there one day.

For now, I will have faith. For now, *I will have faith.*

Hold On

When you are at your lowest, hold on to this.

Hold on to the positivity, light and happiness that others always bring. Hold on to the beautiful memories that make you wish you could go back in time. Hold on to the dreams that you had and the ones that came true. Hold on to every memory of when things worked out even when you expected that they never would. Hold on to your family, your friends, and your loved ones. Hold on to the teachings, and the experiences – even if they bring you pain. Hold on to your heart, your soul and every emotion that you've ever felt. Hold on to yourself, because you need to. Because you should.

Because if you don't hold on to yourself then how can you expect that someone else would?

Hurting

You've been hurt before, but you don't remember it very well. That place between struggle and hope, light and dark, the past and the present. You've felt sorrow like this before, but the only difference is that it hurt a lot more then. But it doesn't hurt as much anymore.

This is a sign of your strength, and you need to accept it. You need to come to terms with your growth. You need to recognise that people leaving, failure, losing and negative chapters in your life don't hurt you as much as they did before. But just because bad stuff doesn't affect you as much, it doesn't mean that something is wrong with you or that you're not the same person. It means that you've flourished, you've learnt, and you've been empowered. It just means that you are so much more than you were yesterday and all the insight that you've acquired from your past is now demonstrating what you're capable of.

You've been there before – battling between hurting and letting go, between being happy and simmering in sorrow. The only difference is that it doesn't hurt as much as it used to – which is good. Because it means that you've thrived. It means that you've learnt to deal with the pain. It means that you're stronger now than you ever were before.

Small Battles

Sometimes you need to focus on the small battles first. Like peeling off your duvet in the morning and getting out of bed. Like unwrapping the tangled mess of your hair, picking up the brush and getting rid of one knot at a time. Like going to the grocery store to grab not just ice cream but some fruits and vegetables too. And making breakfast, lunch and dinner for yourself. Like switching the lights off and letting a candle flame flicker soft radiance into the room. Like putting your clothes in the laundry and getting in the shower without the thickness in your throat that pushes you to cry as the water streams down your face.

Sometimes you need to ignore other people's progress and focus on your own baby steps. Like meeting up with a friend over coffee and making plans for dinner. Like applying to a new job that you look forward to or leaving your current one. And smiling at your reflection in the mirror and getting dressed each morning – even if you're not going to step out. Like stepping out anyway to take a walk, to get some fresh air, to browse through the aisles of shops and visit cafes that used to bring you joy. Like letting yourself mould back into your previous life, but as a new person with a new perspective.

It's not about jumping head-first into your healing. It's about the tiny actions that you take each day that bring you closer to being warm again. It's not about getting over your past instantly or waking up one morning and being miraculously healed. It's about moving forward, step by step – and as gently as you can. It's about letting your heart mend as slowly as it can, and the only way that it should.

Because at the end of the day, it's about loving yourself no matter how small your progress is on your healing journey. It's about not judging yourself for the big or small steps that you're not able to take. It's about appreciating your effort anyway, because you're giving it your best and *that's all that matters.*

This Will Pass

I know that it's difficult right now. Nothing makes sense and no matter how hard you try – there's nowhere to escape to. But believe me when I tell you that this will pass. This time in your life is preparing you for strength and a transformation that only you can bring about. Remember this, nothing in life lasts forever and just like the good moments in our life, the bad moments pass too. And before you know it, this difficult time in your life will disappear with a quick flutter of your eyelids. The bad moments are like intervals that separate episodes of happiness in your life, which means that even though it seems like nothing will ever be the same again – this is a tiny setback in the bigger journey that you're destined to take.

Believe me when I say that you're going to come out the other end, grateful for all the knowledge, and all the wholesome hurt and healing. Even if you don't see it now. Even if none of it makes sense to you. Even if you would rather pull the covers over your head than slide your eyes over it every now and then to get a glimpse of what life holds for you. You will come through from this. You will see the bigger picture. You will understand the plan set out for you by the natural laws – and you will rise again.

Trust me. You will.

I'm Proud of You

I want you to know that I'm proud of you.

I'm proud of the folds on your cheeks when you smile, because these days I don't see more than a shadow of emotion appear on your face. I'm proud when you greet the morning by pulling back your blinds and letting the sun turn your room yellow, and when you slide into your furry slippers, soft and cold under your warm feet, ready to let them take you downstairs. I'm proud that even though life hasn't been kind to you recently, you still show up, ready to face each day with a warrior's grace. I'm proud that you haven't let life topple you over completely.

I'm proud that, despite all the reasons why, you still haven't given up. I'm proud that even if life crashes around you again, you will get back up once more. Even if you take a little while to do so or don't want to, even if this time moving on is harder than before – you will, and I'm proud of you because of it. I'm proud that you express what you're going through a lot more these days. I'm proud that you let the tears gush out, pushing your head back and closing your eyes firmly to welcome them as they come. I'm proud when you wipe those very tears away, with a slight glimmer of hope on your face – a knowing look that your heart is getting washed of all the pain.

I'm proud that you haven't given up on yourself, even though I know how badly you wanted to. I'm proud that you're still pushing through your path to self-discovery and you're still moving forward, no matter how heavily, slowly or painfully. I know that this isn't what you wanted. But I'm proud that you're still holding on. I'm so proud of you.

Dear Self

Losing attachments is a part of life.

Those of you who read this book in a linear manner already know that one of the ways in which I found myself was through friendship. As I battled through the post-heartbreak stage in my life, I met some beautiful people and made incredible friends who showed me how beautiful unconditional love was. They were wonderful souls who valued my existence.

For someone like me who's struggled with her self-worth her whole life – these people arrived as a blessing, brightening up my dimming life and enabling me to understand what was right for me.

Inevitably, when a friendship is built on one-sided feelings, it gets hard to pursue. Unfortunately, I found myself in two of these. I was incredibly close to two magnificent boys – who brought with them lots of warmth with them on my healing. They were great friends that I had the good fortune of meeting and learning from. And I never thought that I would lose either of them. I had some of the most memorable moments in my life when they were there, and I guess I took their presence in my life for granted. Because nothing lasts forever, and even though I believed that our friendship would never fall apart – eventually it did. And I lost them both. And as difficult as it is to drink down this truth – just like the bad times pass you by, so do the good – it's one we need to accept if we want to keep moving forward in our lives.

It all came out of the blue. Suddenly. Unexpectedly.

But I can't say that subconsciously I didn't see it coming. Blurry parts meshed together slowly to form the reality that none of us would be happy with the situation going forward. And as much as the friendship with both of these boys meant to me, the strong attachment that I developed towards the friend that I had feelings for inevitably led me to have the same low self-esteem that I'd left behind long ago. I couldn't let myself fall into a black hole once more. And it's for this reason that I decided to prioritise myself by breaking the first of my two friendships. And to prioritise his self-worth and put himself first – my second friend broke it off with me.

So, there I was, after some of the most incredible and life-altering chapters in my life, mourning the loss of two invaluable friends whom I couldn't maintain a close connection with any longer. And I'm certain that you've all formed attachments at various points in your life, so you might have an idea of how difficult it is to move on from people that you speak to every day. These are people that you share your adventures with, that you laugh, cry, joke and make memories with.

It is hard. It is unbelievably hard.

The first few days are swelled with uncomfortable adjustment. Adjusting to looking at your phone after you wake up and not finding a, *'Good Morning'*, message flashing across the screen. Adjusting to not having someone to message every few hours to tell them about your day, about the latest gossip at work and what you had for lunch, and the tiny jokes that you used to toss back and forth over a virtual net as the hours passed. Adjusting to scrolling through your Instagram feed and not being able to send them funny memes that used to plant a smile on their face. Adjusting to not calling them on your way home from work, to work, to grab some food, to meet up with friends, or when you're alone in your room and need someone to speak to.

Having to adjust is so difficult.

Your fingers practically shake to send them a text and ask how they are, or to admit defeat and call them to apologise – whether or not you were the one who left to begin with. After the torment of the first few days, you start to tell yourself that it might be better to have them as a friend in your life – even though it's bruising to be *'just friends'* with them – because you've seen how difficult life is without them. You can't take it anymore. You just can't. You need them back in your life and you will do whatever it takes to make sure that this happens.

That's the issue with forming attachments. When you get to know someone, you can't fathom how close your relationship (platonic or not) will be. You continue speaking to this person, having your banter via social media, then move it forward to

WhatsApp and phone conversations until they become an unmissable part of your life. Then, you wake up and realise that your day doesn't start unless you've texted them in the morning and the hours feel naked without a few exchanges with them. But we don't grasp the strength of our attachments until we stop talking to those people. Then, it hits us like a clear glass window that we walk smack-bang into – because we couldn't see it properly. Or we did see it but chose to ignore it and secretly prayed that it wasn't there when we walked into it.

The point is – *attachments suck.*

When you stop speaking to those that you're attached to – without a steady network of family and friends to keep you busy – you inevitably fall into the pit of loneliness. That's what happened to me. I lost two close friends in the short space of a week. I couldn't find solace in my other friends/family to recover from it soon enough. And the fact that one of them had been an integral part of my day for the last 1.5 years added to the weight of difficulty that hung over me. Both of them had been extremely valuable to me and perhaps if I'd lost just one, I would've been able to find peace by talking to the other *(as bad as that sounds)*. But I lost them both at the same time. The first one through my desire to put myself first. And the second one through his desire to put himself first.

Looking back – I can't blame anyone for it.

We all had wishes that were at odds with one another, so we did what any rational adult would do – we removed ourselves from a situation that had the potential to become truly toxic.

It'd already gotten as a bad as it could, and for those of you who read the section titled, 'The time I broke the heart of someone I deeply cared about', you've probably realised that this friend is the same person. He removed himself from my life because he'd had enough. And I removed myself from my other friend's life because I – like my former friend – also had enough.

The biggest difficulty in putting yourself first is coming to terms with why you did it when it's tormenting you incontestably.

When you're sitting all alone in your bedroom, watching the minutes tick by as you scroll aimlessly through your phone, or miserably stare out the window, you start to question everything that's wrong with your life. This begins with the decision that you made to leave someone you really cared about. A kernel of anxiety develops in your mind as you skim through past conversations, unticking favourited messages on your WhatsApp where they made you laugh, smile, or blush fiercely. Frantic with worry over whether you will find someone else who will be this easy to get along with – you churn over whether you should message them again.

Loneliness after losing an attachment is real.

Regardless of whether it was a romantic or unromantic relationship. When you send them your last message, remove them from all social media platforms and block their number – loneliness blows you in the face with all its rage. This applies the other way around to. When the other person, who decided to remove you from their life, takes you off social media, blocks your number and doesn't give you any closure – you feel *(and rightly so)* personally attacked. Loneliness creeps in like a dark shadow. It keeps knocking on the door where your peace resides, waiting for you to let it in so it can feel at home inside your head and stay there for as long as it wants.

Being alone in this way welcomes a lot of other negative emotions too – low self-esteem and self-worth, self-rejection and all other emotions/beliefs that rely on you for their flourishment. When you're this lonely, you're not sure what to do with yourself. You went from having a bustling social life – days laced with friendly banter, laughter and ease – to a cold solitariness that you're not used to. Up until then, you were confident that you don't need other people to be happy. You thought that you were one of those strong, independent individuals who found love and peace in themselves and other people *merely added to it.* Other people weren't the reason for your fulfilled, wonderful life. They were healthy additions, the kind that you could live easily without. *You didn't need them.* But you were happy that they were there.

The first lesson that coming out of an attachment teaches you is this; no matter how immune you think that you are to attachment with others, once people leave – you come to terms with how much you relied on them for the *'normal functioning'* of your life.

The most precious piece of wisdom that you can gain when you're in this place is how to *come home to yourself.* Being alone – where you remove yourself from essential people in your life, or they remove themselves from you – allows you to re-evaluate the core value that you have picked up time and time again – *other people cannot become the sole reason for your happiness.* You came to grips with this in the past when you broke your heart. You faced it again when you got to know more people and they left. And, once more, the bleak reality is before you: you need to stop attaching your happiness to other people.

I know that it's easier said than done. But this whole experience of losing two of the most important friends in my life opened my eyes wide to the existence of temporality.

The truth is that everything is temporary.

Our jobs, education, gadgets, routine, relationships, health. Our lives. This world. What gives meaning to our existence is *believing that nothing is.* Our jobs are more meaningful when we tell ourselves that we will have them forever. We wake up with a drive each morning, determined to beat yesterday's targets because it gives our today a purpose. Our gadgets appear valuable when they're more expensive, guaranteed to last us a lifetime and if not, then at least expendable enough to be replaced with better gadgets. Our relationships – with our parents, friends and lovers – appear to be everlasting. Your parents will always be your parents, and love is supposed to last forever, isn't it? And friendships are made for lifetimes, right? *Wrong.*

The existence of those very people is contingent, let alone your relationship with them. Sure, your parents will always be your parents, but the time that you have with them is limited. As with your friends and lovers – a very minimal number of these relationships last as long as we do.

How is this in any way related to attachments and the loneliness that comes after they break?

Simply put, as long as you believe that everything lasts forever, you will be miserable when you lose those things – whether it's a job, a relationship, a lover or a dear one. The pain that you experience after you lose those invaluable relationships/achievements will be unbearable. But when you accept that everything in life is temporary – the separation of people, the loss of jobs and the departure of your loved ones – it will feel less like your whole world is falling apart when they end. Instead, you will view those departures the way that they're meant to be viewed– as an unavoidable characteristic of a meaningfully contingent life.

You will still be affected when friendships break, when lovers leave and when, misfortunately, your loved ones pass away. You will be grief-stricken. The anxiety will be there, and no one can take that away. Because without essential attachments and relationships, our lives lose all meaning. But when you string together the truth that *important relationships add value to your life* with the truth that *nothing lasts forever* – loss becomes bearable. It becomes less about your self-esteem (*you're not good enough for the job, the friend or the lover*) and more about the shifting pattern of life and the importance of change that varying relationships and loss enable us to undergo.

Losing people then becomes *essential* for your development rather than a *hindrance* to it.

This is how I dragged myself away from self-pity and swam out of the pool of loneliness. It didn't happen overnight. The first few weeks were terribly hard. I couldn't sleep. I couldn't eat. I couldn't get through an entire day without replaying what happened in my mind, trying to figure out what went wrong, trying to uncover how I could fix it, how I could convince them to be my friends again – even though I was the one who ended one of those friendships.

But as I came to terms with the temporality of life – through several conversations with my other friends and family – I acknowledged that whatever happened was for the best. It had nothing to do with my self-worth. It had nothing to do with what I did or didn't deserve. It had nothing to do with how good/bad my actions were – well, to an extent anyway. I say this because actions will cause reactions and sometimes the reaction is undesirable – such as my friend leaving – but this doesn't mean that my initial actions were wrong. It means that my actions didn't fall in accordance with what my friend wanted, which is why he left. In the same way, my other friend's actions caused me to leave and it doesn't mean that he did something wrong or that I did.

It just means that we both did what was *right for us both.*

This doesn't make me a bad human – it makes me (and both my friends) *human.* Those friendships ended because they had an expiry date. They weren't meant to last forever. I wish that they did but those people were only supposed to play that long *(or short)* a part in my life. As was I. We wouldn't have added any more value to each other's lives if we stayed friends for longer – all we would have done is contribute to the discomfort that we were already experiencing. Those friendships were meant to fall apart when they did. And none of us could have stopped it from happening.

The loneliness that I felt afterward was predictable. It couldn't be helped. But when I look back at it now, I see those friendships as what they were truly – overwhelming attachments. And these can only weaken you. They can only push you to rely on other people for what you can give yourself – love, peace, laughter and joy. This doesn't mean that you shouldn't enjoy other people's company. It doesn't mean that you must live as a nomad *(unless you want to)*. It also doesn't mean that attachments are a hindrance to your growth.

What it means is that the loneliness you experience after an attachment breaks will eventually disappear. *It has to.* Because attachments are contingent. And once the invisible string that was connecting you to them weakens – you observe the foundation of your friendship/relationship for what it truly was. And this is what enables you to find comfort in being alone after those relationships break.

Eventually I, too, learned what my friendship with those two boys truly meant. I wasn't supposed to consider those broken attachments as a setback – in fact, they contributed to my growth. I wasn't meant to fall down, feel sorry for myself and let loneliness overwhelm me forever – which is part of grieving a lost friendship – I was supposed to gain strength from it. Which I did. I twisted my head back, investigated the metaphorical tornado of memories that I created with those two before turning to face my future. After then, I only remembered them with a reminiscent smile on my face for all the good times that we shared without getting upset over how it all fell apart.

Because the truth is, I didn't lose anything when I lost them.

Instead, I was equipped with a different perception, a lifetime of memories and the power to keep loving myself as I continued the path that I was on before them. Those two friends were precious to my healing and were the reason behind much of the sunshine in my life, but when it was time – I had to put on a brave face and keep walking without them.

After all, this journey was mine to take and mine only.

Temporary

I always tell myself that the new year brings with it hope, light and a better future. But now I understand how much of that depends on us. Embracing change is a huge part of moving forward. And stepping away from our comfort zone into new challenges is what builds a better future for us. And hope and light – well, that arrives when we expand our heart and soul wide enough to let glimmers of sunshine stream into our lives and stay.

Sunshine arrives with people, adventures and love, and it truly makes a difference when we let those intermittent particles of happiness impact the overall quality of our life into a positive and fulfilling one.

This day, this month and this year are all temporary. Just like tomorrow, next month and next year will be. Nothing stays the same, and that's the truth. The only difference is the mindset that we take forward with us. The only difference is that we couldn't change yesterday and only learn from it, but we have the power to influence our tomorrow. The only difference is that even if everything is temporary, we can still impact this temporarily magnificent world. The only difference is that we – as humans – can still live forever; in the form of memories, lessons, smudges in the background of other people's best experiences, and as lovers, carers and friends.

The only difference is that yesterday made us who we are today, but what we do today decides who we will be tomorrow.

And this is powerful. Life doesn't stay the same and we shouldn't either.

That's what I'm taking forward with me. I'm taking forward the dreams in my eyes, as well as my family, my friends, and the love that cradles my heart. I'm taking forward the memories of yesterday that make my soul raw with affection. I'm taking forward the vast adventures that I've had, the ones that have stretched throughout my life, and the memories of when I've loved, lost and gained.

I'm taking it all forward with me.

Because even if everything is temporary and the future is undecided – what I have today is magnificent. It is worth living for. It belongs to me. And this is what I'm taking forward with me into the new year.

Healing

Healing isn't a destination; *it is a process.*

You will find this out after you take the journey for a while. You will have made progress. Your heart won't hurt as much. You will smile wholeheartedly and enjoy the company of others, and you will look forward to life. But suddenly – a photo might flash before your eyes, or a song that sends you plummeting back into the past will play in the background, sending shivers through your spine. It will make sense to you then – that healing isn't straightforward. It is messy. It's uncomfortable and it may bring with it some of the hardest tests that you've had to take. You might have to swallow some bitter pills and tend to your own wounds, because that's how lonely healing can sometimes be.

But, believe me – *it will be okay.*

Healing isn't easy – but that's the beauty of it. You will face battles that will prepare you for strength, and for life. You will learn to be soft in new ways. You will become gentle with yourself before you extend that gentleness to others. You will also become strong and powerful. You will be patient and kind. You will learn new things about yourself and learn to accept all your vulnerabilities and scars.

Healing will give you all the invaluable tools that will contribute to the betterment of your life. And you will grow, love – *you will grow.* All you need to do is have faith in the process of healing and know that even if it takes time, even if it tests your will, and even if you never reach the destination that you had in mind – you will reach where you were always meant to be.

That's the beauty of healing and that's why you should trust the process and welcome the journey with open arms. Because healing is a process, one that will change your entire life forever – if only you gave it a chance.

Being Alone

You can be alone for as long as you like, but you will never truly be comfortable in solitude until you welcome it with open arms.

Nothing prepared me for the peace that I felt after several years of being alone. It was a wintry Sunday morning, the water was icy on my fingertips as I splashed it over my face, causing tiny shrieks to leave me, and I lifted my head up to see my reflection in the mirror. I'm not sure whether it was the aura of that day, the cold water jilting me awake, or the ease with which the weekend had passed me by – but I was happy. Calm. *I was better than okay.*

I'd been alone for years before that and continued to remain alone even after that day. It wasn't like I had just become single. It was the only life I'd ever known. I often took pride in my ability to not need someone to *'complete me'* or validate my existence. Yes, there was the honeyed comfort of family and friends, and the infectious laughter of my loved ones kept me going – but I had never lived life as another person's *'half'*.

I had always tried to be whole on my own.

Spending most of your years alone teaches you a lot of things – both good and bad. Like how to sprinkle your time on people who have the potential to love you before realising how much of a waste that was – because they couldn't live up to that potential. How there isn't a *'Good Morning'* or *'Good Night'* waiting for you before you hit bed or get up. How everyone, but you, seems to have found the person they were looking for, and you can't chase away the thought that perhaps there's something wrong with you. How you keep telling everyone, *'I'm okay being single'*, when really, at the back of your mind you're jokingly questioning whether you're going to die alone. And how, no matter what others say, you don't know whether someone out there is truly meant for you.

But being alone teaches you the most important lessons.

Like how to be resilient and to never bow down to another, to never *'settle'* because you're afraid of loneliness or accept a love that's not enough because you think that this is all you're going to get. It teaches you to have faith in your heart, to trust your emotions and to be there for yourself when you need it the most. It teaches you to ask yourself where you'd like to eat, what colour would suit your nails and which park you want to go running in. It teaches you to rely on your own views about what's right or wrong for you, and to carve your own path towards dreams that don't depend on someone else to complete them.

Being alone teaches you to accept what's meant for you and to push away whatever isn't. It teaches you to welcome every fragment of yourself in its entirety, and to not pluck out your vulnerabilities as imperfections but as gems that make you more loveworthy.

Yes, there are lonely nights, nights when you wish you were speaking to someone with love bubbling in their heart for you. There are also moments of disorientation where you're not sure where you're headed because the person who's supposed to be with you still seems like a blur far in the future.

But there is also security, a sense of belonging and peace. There is also the feeling of being at home with yourself that you will never find anywhere else. There's consistency, safety and self-reliance. There's the undeniable truth that there may or may not be someone beside you one day, but your heart and soul will still be there. You will still be there. Your dreams and hopes will still be there. The faith that you have in yourself will still be there.

Being alone teaches you so much, but the biggest lesson I've taken from it is this – someone else could pour their all into you and it still won't be enough if you're not already whole, if you're not already a complete person when they meet you. And that's the truth.

Being alone means admitting that you have to be your own knight-in-shining armour and save yourself every time and in every way that you wish someone else would. Being alone teaches you that the right person is going to *add more* to your already meaningful life, they're not going to *give meaning to* it.

Let go of fear and embrace being alone.

It's weird, isn't it? Someone else's presence can change your life for better or worse. You get used to them for weeks, months and years until one day, they leave – causing you unbearable pain. Their departure feels like you've lost a part of yourself too. Emptiness engulfs you after they're gone. You're unsure of what to do. Where to go? You don't remember what your life looked like before they came and now that they're gone – you've lost all sense of normalcy in your life.

Who do you turn to for the care that they gave you?

Who do you rely on when you need an outlet or a shoulder to cry on?

Who do you reach out to when you want to forget all your problems for a little while?

As each day wears on, you grasp how much you depended on this person: for your smiles, your pep talks and your deep conversations about life. For your laughter and all the big and small moments that made life *life* for you.

I was like that too and if I were to lose someone again in the future, I would be grief-stricken and upset all over again. Because it's natural to slip into – *loneliness*. Especially after experiencing loss.

Loss brings out different shades of sorrow in your life that can plague you with all kinds of dark emotions. Emotions that you weren't capable of feeling before, as well as poisonous thoughts that you never knew you held. And the hard truth is that when you're in this place of loneliness – you feel it resentfully. You tell yourself that there's no one in the world who feels the way that you do. No one else can understand you, support you or comfort you. No one else knows that you're going through.

The truth is – *loneliness is a very lonely feeling.*

It detaches you from the outside world where you almost picture yourself watching everyone through a glass window, with no means to escape and join them.

But this isn't true. You're not alone in feeling alone. We've all been there. Because we've all experienced thoughts hammering a nail inside our head, framing our mind with dark ideas, indignant ideas, aggrieved ideas – telling us that we have no one, that we have nowhere to escape to, that we don't matter and we will be left all alone and no one will come to our rescue.

Many of us have been in that place and I'm one of them. It's not a pleasant place to be in. Your reality becomes a deep dark well, without a rope to climb up, without someone to scream to for help, without a glimmer of light, indicating a way out.

Loneliness can arise for various reasons – such as when you try to distance yourself from people, when someone in your life leaves or passes away or when your heart breaks. Some actions that you take for the betterment of your mental health can end up making it worse before it gets better – because the loneliness that follows this separation crowds you with gloom.

Even though this normally comes after someone significant leaves, it doesn't mean that loneliness always arises after departure/separation. Sometimes, loneliness stems when you're with people that you love. Sometimes, loneliness erupts after the most eventful day of your life, taking you by surprise – *or shock* – and changing the direction of your entire day. Sometimes, loneliness appears with a quick blink of an eye while you're having some of the most significant months or years of your life. Sometimes, loneliness flows in gently, remaining dormant for a long time – infecting your peace of mind – until it makes itself visible to you out of nowhere.

The truth is, there's no clear-cut path for loneliness, nor is there an empty space in your life that it settles down in. In the same way, there's no transparent solution or a route that you can follow to come out of loneliness.

A good thing to take away from this is to know – with certainty – that you aren't alone in how you feel. You really aren't. Innumerable people experience loneliness. So many people battle with it for years before reaching a brighter, steadier place in life. You can remove yourself from this toxic place too, if you wish to. *'But how?'*, you think. Loneliness is heavy on your heart and you might not know how to remove it, and I understand that, because I felt it too.

I'm not sure exactly how I dragged myself out of the hole of loneliness that I found myself in. Honestly, I'm not. But what I am sure of is this – when I started to embrace my own company wholeheartedly, being alone no longer felt like a punishment. Instead, *it was a gift*. Because over time, I understood that my loneliness stemmed from my reliance on other people. I depended on them for a good time, for a laugh, for soulful conversations, for company while I ate out at my favourite restaurant, as an escape from my house whenever it became overwhelming, and as an escape from myself.

In the initial stages of moving on – I didn't like spending more than a few minutes alone in my room. The moment there was an air of quiet, the monsters in my head would start rumbling like clothes in a dryer, twisting my insides with anxiety and fear that this was all that I was ever going to be – *miserable and alone*. To escape those irrationalities, I would watch Netflix, turn on the TV, listen to loud music or go downstairs and sit with my family (even though mentally I wasn't with them). I did everything in my power to escape the silence that awaited me in my room.

I was playing a game of cat and mouse with myself. I was running away from my thoughts and deep down I knew that until I didn't stop, until I didn't reach the dead end of the gloomy alleyway of loneliness that I found myself in and turn around to face my monsters – I would never be comfortable in being alone.

So, that is just what I did. I stopped running.

I stopped letting my monsters chase me.

I stopped hurling different ideas at my mind to fill it with stuff so there was no room for my anxieties to roam free. And I welcomed them. I opened my arms, my heart and my attention wide to let all those emotions, judgements and ideas in and I plucked them apart – one by one – to deal with them.

The basis of irrational thoughts such as these is in the name – they're *irrational*. When you start reasoning with yourself, when you question those ideas that raise red flags against your self-worth, you realise that there is no reasoned argument there. Those thoughts only stem from fear. Fear of being alone. Fear of never being loved. Fear of not being enough. Fear of everyone finding out who you truly are and hating you. Fear of not knowing who you are to begin with. Fear of all your happiness being taken away from you.

Fear is irrational. It doesn't have a basis to stand on.

Fear doesn't depend on reason or a cluster of reasons. Instead, it drinks out of your vulnerabilities and sucks all the strength from your trauma to feign the appearance of rationalism – but it truly isn't. When you let fear control you, you become a puppet to your innermost weak thoughts. You let *your mind tell you* what's right or wrong for you rather than the other way around. As a result, you start pushing yourself away. You stop valuing yourself. After all that's happened, how could you?

How could you possibly assume that you've done anything good in your life?

All of this is fear talking. It's not you. It's not what you truly feel.

If you're letting your mind control you, you start considering all those toxic views that are fatal for your thriving and wellbeing. You start pushing yourself away and grasp onto other people to give you everything that – in all honesty – should be dependent on you.

But the moment you look those fears in the eye and wave them off like the annoying flies that they are – blurring your clear view of the world – you're able to grasp that there's no place for fear where there is growth. Where there is peace. Where there is comfort. There is no place for fear where there's happiness. And you need to start believing that what is yours is meant to be yours. More importantly, believe that even if other people leave – you still deserve happiness, love and care because it comes from you. You must get rid of fear in order to embrace yourself. You must get rid of fear if you want to be comfortable in being alone, if you want to be happy in being alone. You must get rid of fear if you want to be free.

And that's what I did. I considered all my fears, one by one, and I understood that they had no bearing on me. They were meaningless, illogical entities that could only bring me down if I let them. And in the end, I didn't let them. I snatched the reigns back to my life and I told fear that there was no place for it over here.

That is what I want you to do. I want you to take the seed of fear and grind it under your feet. Especially when it comes to the loneliness that you feel after experiencing loss.

I know that it kills when someone leaves. It feels like it's the end of the world but truthfully – it isn't. In fact, it's the beginning of your world. Anything other than that is fear telling you that you won't be able to survive without them. But you survived without them before, right? When they weren't in your life and you were still living, laughing and loving? When you weren't in possession of their number, didn't have them on social media or even know their name? But still – you lived as gracefully and adventurously as you could.

You've had your heart broken many times before this. You lost so many people. Friends. Family. Colleagues. People who promised you that they would always be there for you. But just like everyone does – they left too. And you survived because you knew that you would. You got back up and looked at all your doubts and insecurities and you proved them wrong by falling in love with life again, by falling in love with love again.

This time is no different. This loneliness is no different to the one that you've felt before. What's stopping you from embracing solitude is the fear that still has power over you. And you need to stop letting fear tell you what you are/are not entitled to. Stop letting fear scare you into believing that all the good in your life will be over before you know it. Stop letting fear determine the strength of your joy and your love. And stop letting fear choose how difficult it will be for you to move on from this. Only you know how difficult/easy it will be and deep down you know how much courage you have within you to look at your vulnerabilities and turn them into your strengths.

You are worthy of love. Especially your own love.

Embrace being alone. Enjoy it. Take yourself out on walks. Grab a coffee. Slip into the plumpest sofa in a gently thrumming, dim-lit café at the edge of a street lined with shops and people, the kind that looks like it's been taken out of a postcard of a beautiful foreign village. Watch people mill about outside while you unpeel yourself on the inside to learn more about what you want and what you need. Get on a plane and travel the world by yourself. Spend as much time in silence as you can and let your mind wander to beautiful, calm places. And if it doesn't, if you find splutters of darkness making their way into your thoughts – listen to them. Understand them. Try to figure them out. What are they trying to tell you and how can you turn them into a beautiful aura of light?

Let your emotions flow out of your heart and be attentive to them. Listen to the beating of your chest and hear what it has to say. You have the power to give your heart whatever it needs. Have faith in yourself. Consider the beauty of solitude. It is a gift, if anything. Once you stop letting fear rule your life – you will welcome solitude. This will transform your definition of living and loving forever.

Take the Time You Need

Don't feel bad if you need time off from everyone for your mental/emotional wellbeing. Don't beat yourself up about cancelling on your friends or saying no to your family because you don't have the energy to go out. Don't give yourself a hard time because you need to vent to those that you confide in – you're not dampening anyone's mood. Stop telling yourself that your problems are a burden to those who love you, or that you're bringing negativity to them because you're not happy right now.

If you need to talk about what you're going through – then don't stop yourself. Talk about it. If you need some time away from everyone to come to terms with your emotions, then take that necessary space away from it all. If you don't want to go out, no matter how much they ask you to, then don't – especially if you're not happy. You don't need to do the anything that you don't want to just because it's expected of you. Focus on yourself. On your wellbeing. And on your own betterment.

And I promise you – *it will all fall into place.*

Adventures

Go on adventures.

Adventures that wake you up and – by that – I mean *truly wake you,* where in the morning it's not just your eyes that open but your soul too. Adventures that enlighten you; to new cities bursting with energy and people with kind hearts who like to make small talk about the weather and the city they grew up in and where their journey has taken them until now, and the stuff that makes their eyes crease as they smile. Try new food; dishes that scares you and look different but taste just as delicious as your favourite meal back home. Take yourself on walks, alone, with a friend or a group of people – both old and new – who feel like home and add to the peace in your life.

Take risks. Trail down difficult paths that lead to unknown destinations and welcome the perspective that those trips bring. Hike up tall mountains and hitch hike all the way down. Talk to strangers, discover a little bit about them and what energises them and let them discover a little bit about you too. Welcome your growth with each passing day. Observe how much you adapt as each new adventure brings with it a world of knowledge. How each new place – *no matter how foreign* – can teach you more about yourself and how, no matter how far you travel into the curves of the world, you will always find your way back. Trust me, you will.

Go on adventures. As many as you want to and can go on. Travel as far as your feet take you, even if it's down the street to a shop you've never visited before or all the way on the other side of the world. And at the end of each new adventure that you take, watch how much value it brings to your life overall.

It is Okay

It's okay to start again. It's okay to change your mind about decisions that you were sure of before – because you've changed. Because you've seen life in countless ways that now reflect your growth back at you. You're not the same person you were weeks, months and years ago.

It's okay to walk on a timeline that is different to others. Because it's no less than theirs. It's not behind anyone else's and it's not ahead either – *it is yours*. Your timeline is unique and special to you. So, embrace it. It's okay to watch old jobs, friendships and goals fall out of your grasp while other goals, people and relationships fall into it. Welcome the journey, with every sharp hill that you cross and every soft bend that you take to get to where you want to be – even if you're unsure about where that is. Even if you don't want to foresee the long voyage that awaits you and focus on the small road ahead, in the shape of hours, days or weeks that unwind before you – that is still okay.

The point is – you can choose to slow down, or you can choose to fasten your pace, and one choice is no bigger or better than the other. The choice depends on your personal battle. It's okay to take a break. It's okay to take a breather. It's okay to give up and start all over again. It's okay to decide when something isn't meant for you and it's okay to decide when it is. Just focus on yourself.

But don't injure hearts or create wars in other people's lives. Don't become selfish in the name of *'self-love'* and don't wrap yourself with jealousy, competition or bitterness. Don't intentionally cause others pain or upset them. Keep your eyes on your timeline. On your life. On what you need and what you deserve and spread love and light wherever you go.

Trust me – it is okay to focus on yourself.

It is okay to put yourself first.

It is okay.

Blessings

The truth is, we don't know how many blessings we've had in the form of heartache and losses. We don't know who had to break us for us to learn to cherish our hearts, who had to push us down for us to gain the strength to get back up on our own and who had to leave us behind for us to recognise that this journey is ours and we're most powerful when we take it alone.

'We all play a part in giving each other invaluable lessons.'

The truth is, we don't know how many people became the teachings in our lives that allowed us to become more courageous and wiser. We don't know which falls we took that grounded us and which pushes we felt that led us to where we are today. We must appreciate – in the subtlest sense – each person who has stayed or gone, even those who bring up tears at the back of our eyes when we remember our time with them. Even those who cause our throats to become thick with hurt. Even those who cause a bubble of anger to rise in our chest. Even those whom we don't want to think about because our ache is too raw. Because we don't know how many of them were cloaked angels that gave us the biggest wins in the form of rejections.

We don't know how many of them were good spirits disguised as imperfect, tarnished humans who had to wound us, leave us behind and let us go in order for us to embrace ourselves and keep heading towards the life that was always meant for us.

Every time something goes wrong, I look for the learning or the blessing.

When I was knee-deep in the quicksand of sadness, drowning relentlessly and anxious that I'll never be able to get out – I couldn't find any learning in the pain that I was experiencing. I couldn't grasp what the purpose of being this miserable was. This distress wasn't going to bring me any goodness. Not now. Not in the future. Not ever. There was no way that hurting this much was okay for my heart or my soul. There was no way that crying this much was okay for my sanity. It couldn't be. *It just couldn't.*

My mental health was in shambles. My career was a mess. My friendships were unsecure, scattered and worsened my emotional state. My skin was disastrous; I had fat red spots all over my face which I tried everything in my power to get rid of but couldn't. I cried myself to sleep each night and woke up with my face pressed against a damp pillow in the morning. I couldn't recall what early hours in the morning my tears melted into a penetrating, uncomfortable slumber. I was easily irritable, gave dull responses and refused to step out of the house unless I really had to. I couldn't plant a fake smile on for anyone. I was certain that most people in my life could figure out what was going on with me based on just my appearance and behaviour. I was so drained that I felt like a damp, used teabag. The kind that had nothing left to give.

Worst of all – I couldn't even pretend to be okay anymore. I didn't want to go out. I didn't want to stay in. Being in my room for longer than 10 minutes would bring out the waterworks and self-indulged misery. Being in a room filled with people would make me want to leave instantly and go back to my gloom. To escape from my surroundings, I would turn to Instagram and – to my horror – find people in love, getting engaged and married, taking wonderful steps on the career ladder, starting degrees, having babies, voyaging on holidays and having the time of their lives while I was cooped up in my own remorse, mourning the loss of something that never belonged to me.

How could I find a message in everything that I was experiencing?

My life was all over the place, and if someone came along and told me that all those agonising moments were in truth a 'blessing', I would have pounced on them with what little energy I had left. How could it have been a blessing?

How could it, when each day was breaking me brick by brick until – in the end – there would be nothing left of me? How could it, when my personal life was chaotic? How could it, when I had no true friends whom I could rely on?

I couldn't even tell my family what was going on.

And all the goals I'd set for myself had grinded to dust. There was no lesson or blessing in any of this. *I refused to believe it.*

When you're struggling in this way, it's challenging to find a message or a blessing in anything. You don't have the right perspective, or a clear perspective at all. You're wearing the lens of heartache, grief and self-pity and you're seeing the world through this heavily coated, almost blinding view which only brings your own misery to the fore. But you're not entirely wrong in how you feel. You're not wrong when you tell yourself that this is the worst possible place to be in – *because it's pretty bad.* You're not wrong when those spiteful thoughts scurry through your heavy mind as you try to peel your eyes away from yet another happy couple, happy family and happy person with a job and goals and friends while knowing the truth that some – or all – of those failed you. Again.

How could you see the bright side to any of this?

Hurt and anger hang in the air like thick exhaust fumes, creating an exhausting bubble of sadness around you. It's not easy to rip that suffocating bubble open and set yourself free. Unless you're some self-appreciating warrior who's taught themselves to search for a meaning behind all the battles they face. For the rest of us – *we learn* to find blessings in what we've undergone. It doesn't come to us straight away. Then, we take that forward with us and view the world – and everything that we encounter after that – in a new way altogether. We remove the glasses of self-pity and slip on a new set of glasses, or perhaps none at all – encompassing a well-rounded view of our life; along with the knowledge of how much we are yet to experience. Because we understand that being human and experiencing life – both the pleasant and unpleasant aspects – come hand-in-hand. This new perspective is what allows us to see the good in all the bad.

Looking for a lesson in all the good and bad isn't an instinct that we're born with. It's not a part of the syllabus at school – even though it should be. It's not one of the lessons that our parents teach us, unless we're one of those incredibly lucky kids who experienced a healthy, cultivating childhood with two parents who were blissfully in love/cordial and passed down good moral values that they then took forward with them.

Some of us weren't blessed with a childhood of this sort. Some of us scuttled through our broken homes to find remains of love between the rubble of broken glass – the aftermath of yet another unresolved fight, yet another catalyst for the buckets of tears that we would experience later. Some of us weren't taught what's right/wrong by parents who sat us down with their index finger pointing towards a metaphorical blackboard of instructions. Instead – we had to figure out what's right/wrong by observing their mistakes, then making lots of our own. Some of us never witnessed a healthy relationship, or even a healthy life for that matter.

It's for this reason that we keep settling for less in our careers, goals and relationships. It's for this reason that we won't fight when we experience injustice or ill-treatment. It's for this reason that we don't strive for more – more love, more happiness, more peace. It's for this reason that we keep falling for the same genre of people, with false promises of love on their lips and nothing in their hearts for us. People who need to be fixed more than their silent promises to fix us. People who come from homes as broken as ours and hearts more vacant than the one we offer them. Yes, we were broken before they came but they're broken in a different way altogether, and not in a way that we – or they – can fix. Not in a way that won't destroy us if we try. Their brokenness is different to ours and unfortunately, because of our inability to recognise what good or bad love is, we keep falling for this dynamic of people without uncovering the blessing when they leave us.

And it's because of this that it takes time.

It takes longer for us to come to terms with the truth that all those years of anguish were – in disguise – our saviours. Those moments protected us from what wasn't meant to be. They led us in the right direction – we just had to open our eyes and embrace it.

You need to learn to look for the meaning behind your experiences.

As much as love, loss and healing are universal – our individual journeys are not. And just like everything else that you've had to recognise for yourself as the fierce individual that you are – even though you refuse to believe it – you need to uncover the blessing in each slice of pain that you're served. This perspective will mould itself into you over time. Because, unfortunately, there's no schoolteacher here to hammer it into your head or a book with all the answers (although, I'm attempting to provide some of them with this one). It's what you need to do for yourself. There aren't any classes to attend, material to read, revision that you must do or an exam at the end which grades your reflectiveness to determine how much wiser you are now. Because it would be absurd to.

Wisdom comes with experience and experience is a result of time passing and – unfortunately – you learn more from hurting than you do from being happy. That's the truth. The prayers that hang between your tongue during the worst moments of your life are deeper than the ones you chant when you're in the best. That is why – *it's only within your power* to find healing in your discomfort.

I figured it out after a year of feeling a loss etched as deep as a bullet in my heart and hurting throughout my childhood before that. There's a blessing in all the struggles that we face – even if we don't want to believe it at the time. I'm not saying that you should be grateful for the agonising nights, or the thumping discomfort in your chest. I'm not saying that the anxiety, the low mood or any of the messy, bad stuff is good for you. It kills. It isn't pleasant and it can break you. What I'm saying is this – you will reach a point in your life where those very emotions will shred to reveal the invaluable insight within them. You will reach a point where the blessings will show themselves to you. You will reach a point where you will be grateful for every ounce of that hard misery that enveloped you like a tornado.

All you need to do is open your heart and mind to let the truth wander in. The clammy lens that you've got on right now will disappear over time to let your vision clear. Have faith, because it will. It won't be until you're laughing as tears stream down your face, screaming at the top of your lungs on a ride or hugging your friend really tight after a lovely night out when you will feel it. You will feel it truly. *And it will be magical.*

The teachings and all the blessings are there but they require the right perspective and lots of healing over time for you to see them. Just hang in there, because they are there. Just hold on. Because life is working in your favour. Even if you don't see it right now – *it is.* And one day, you will see it for yourself.

Fall Apart

Sometimes things go wrong. People leave. Hearts break. Stuff that you didn't want to happen, happens. Experiences that are out of your control hit you like a wall, and there's not much you can do other than allow this phase of life to unravel. In those moments – it's hard to expect that life will be okay again. How can it be, when it's all falling apart? But it has to get better, doesn't it? Bad stuff happens for us to appreciate the good, and often life falls apart because those pieces need to join in a new way – in the way that they were supposed to.

Sometimes, things go wrong because the patterns that existed were too toxic for us to continue. Because we refuse to step out of our comfort zone and consider what's meant for us – the natural laws/higher reality/God; *they make that change for us*. Sometimes, things go wrong because there's no other direction for them to go and challenges are essential for our development. Sometimes, things go wrong because we're trying so hard to push pieces that don't fit together for it all to make sense. But those pieces need to fall apart. We need to fall apart.

Life needs to fall apart.

Only then can it come together the way it was meant to.

Let it Go

Sure, we can't solve all our problems by saying, *'This is toxic, so I'm leaving.'* Because the best action to take in most cases is to sit down and discuss the problem. Listen to their story. Try to understand where they're coming from. Why did they act that way? What was going on in their head? Consider their side before putting yours forward. Maybe they're struggling in their personal life which they haven't discussed before. Perhaps they're going through stress. Grief. Loss. Loneliness. We just don't know. Life is too short to cut people off instantly without working on it. Because you don't know what tomorrow holds.

You can't be certain that you will see them again and, if you don't, would you regret not working it out with them?

Would you feel bad for not letting the issue go?

If the answer is yes, then maybe you need to communicate it. Life is too precious to let chances go by. And love – love is too beautiful to let it slip between your fingers without fighting for it.

The Days That Matter

The only days that matter are the ones where you choose to fight. Days where you strip off every uncertainty and fear until you are naked in your strength. Days where there is a gleam in your eyes and your hands are curled into tight fists because you've had enough of staying quiet, of being told what to do, of accepting half-empty promises and half-hearted confessions of a love that others can't understand. The only days that matter are the ones where you choose yourself unabashedly, cherishing all that you are and not being affected if others don't. Days where you are proud of yourself and your journey, because it shaped you into the person that you are today – a warrior, a fighter.

The only days that matter are the ones where you smile wholeheartedly and feel happiness settle between your bones, days where you won't bend yourself just so other people can make room for you. Instead, you open your arms, your heart and your soul to welcome everyone into your peaceful bubble, because you always have room for more.

The only days that matter are the ones where you live for yourself. Days where you are at ease with the life that you've been blessed with. Days filled with the sun rising in bliss and setting in compassion, and in between there is only warmth, love and friendship.

Those are the days that matter. Because those are the only days that you will end up remembering the most.

What I hope you take from this.

Writing this book hasn't been easy.

One of the reasons for this is because – I'm healing too. Perhaps from the firsts. Or the seconds. Perhaps from the experiences that I had as a child and everything that I experienced, or from the battles that I faced after I grew up. Sometimes it's hard to talk about healing and what it looks like when you're still knee deep in your healing journey. When you're still trying to find your way through it. When you're still battling with anxiety from all those obstacles that you faced growing up and everything else that followed.

Because I'm still moving on too.

From my yesteryears. From who I was. From what I thought love was and towards what I know love is now. It's hard to talk about healing as a journey when I haven't seen the light in a few of my healing

journeys. Because remember – you're not on just one healing journey and you will never stop healing. Some of you have reached softer places in your journey, while others are still crawling through the foetal trenches of heartache and loss, and you have a long way to go before you're out in the fresh air again. And I want you to know that you will be okay. You will. Truly.

Sure, it will take time. Lots of it. It will demand patience from you. Maturity from you. Strength from you. *But you will bloom, love.* You will bloom.

In many other areas of my life, I'm doing well. Honestly, I am.

Especially when I talk about my first heartbreak. I've left that chapter in my life so far behind that sometimes I don't even remember the details. I have to search deep within to find a fleeting memory or image in relation to my heartbreak in order to draw some inspiration from it for you all.

In my other healing journeys, some days still harder than others, and that's okay too.

I always say that a happy life is a mixture of good and bad experiences – where the good outweigh the bad – and my life has finally found that balance. For this, I'm truly grateful. I'd like to believe that a lot of you are okay too and I hope that after reading this – most of you will be too. But I understand how difficult it can be to talk about mending your heart and moving on. Because it's not easy. Not after everything that you've undergone. And I get that. I do. Don't be hard on yourself if you're still struggling and finding it difficult to move on.

I really hope that you're okay and are doing well. But being okay doesn't mean that talking about the past won't bring to the fore a soft twinge in your chest. It doesn't mean that your throat won't catch a pause when you reminisce some of the most difficult periods of your life. It doesn't mean that you won't tear up at old memories, the past, or everything that you lost.

Happiness and sadness aren't as clear as black and white. You can be happy, smiling and enjoying every arch of your life but still acknowledge the truth that sometimes life will suck, and getting through another day will be hard. But this doesn't take away from your happy, healthy life or mean that you're not making progress. It just means that you're human. *That's all.*

I admit that – on occasion – reminiscing my previous wounds is good for me. It's good to come to terms with your own emotional graph while you're writing about it for others. Because, at the end of it all – all we can really do is hope. We can hope for a brighter tomorrow and a happier today. We can hope for love to settle inside the heart between our ribs and stay there, and we can hope to see everything that we've experienced with a brighter perspective. We can hope that our hearts are connected as we take our individual journeys to heal and we can hope that one day – that gorgeous, shimmering day – we're no longer affected by an ounce of the past. That there isn't a tiny glitch in our chest when we think about. Not a single uncomfortable murmur. Nothing.

Honestly, I'm in that place in healing from heartbreak. I don't feel the slightest murmur of pain or discomfort when I remember it. I've thrived. I've experienced so much in that period. I've learned a lot about life. And about love. I can't even remember that girl properly anymore. But when it comes to my other journeys, the ones that have shrouded my entire existence, the ones that I can't get rid of – because it will be like dislocating my soul from body – I have a long way to go until I can be okay again. But I'm fine with that.

I'm slowly mending the fractures in my life and that's what matters the most. I'm making progress. *We all are.*

You reading this book is evidence of you making progress. Of your willingness to talk about sensitive matters, to read them, to let your mind flood back to reveal that mental picture(s) that rattles you. You reading this book and joining me on this jourjey is evidence of how strong you are. How capable you are of prioritising your wellbeing. *And I'm so proud of you.* I really am.

And if you take anything from this book, I hope that you take this – you can face your battles alone, but you don't need to *be alone* when you're facing them. Human connection is important. So, reach out and speak to someone. Make a friend. Dare to go on adventures. Welcome new relationships. Make amends with your family and let love into your life – in every shape and form.

The journey is beautiful when you take it alone, *but you don't have to be alone when you're taking it.* Everyone is different and you need to do what's best for you.

If you ever feel like life is too overwhelming and you need someone to speak to, you can always email me at info@rubydhal.com.

I'm always here for you. Always.

Lots of love,

Ruby Dhal x

About the Author

Ruby Dhal is a British Afghan-Sikh bestselling author, mental health advocate and speaker.

She's written three books on topics various topics, such as; heartbreak, healing, grief, self-love, loss, mental health and moving on. She has a social media following of over 350,000 and her books have made a home for themselves in every corner of the world. Ruby's words have been shared and appreciated by countless celebrities, mentors and self-help coaches as well as other bestselling authors.

After losing her mother at the age of 4, Ruby turned to books as a form of escapism and soon developed a love for reading stories and writing. Her only dream was to be a novelist one day. She completed a Philosophy degree from UCL and an MA in Philosophy from King's College London before joining a team in Children's Services. After witnessing the negative impact of domestic abuse, poor choices and minimal opportunities for young people stuck in the same cycle as their parents, Ruby's only goal was to write a novel that depicts the lives of underprivileged people of colour in a relatable manner to stimulate positive change and create a new dialogue of their lived experiences.

'Dear Self' is Ruby's 4th book and the most interactive. Ruby has taken a self-help approach to allow her readers to receive as much support as they can during some of the most difficult points in their life, and this is profoundly important to Ruby. Ruby's purpose is to make an impact through the power of words and storytelling. She wants her words to make a positive change in the world and impact readers in a way that allows them to flourish. Ruby believes that everyone has a purpose and once you find your purpose, you should follow it with all your heart. Ruby has found her purpose in writing to make a difference. It's for this reason that Ruby is eager to write, share content and continue impacting the world one word at a time.

Presently, Ruby is working on the first draft of her debut novel which she will find a home for in 2021. Ruby believes in writing books that tell honest and uplifting stories that shed light on BAME characters' lives – because theirs are the ones that are the least voiced. Therefore, all of Ruby's stories are raw, real and reflective of the lives of innumerable POC characters.

Ruby also has a travelling/lifestyle page on Instagram (@r.dhalblogger) which she created to share her passion for travelling, food and books along with nuggets of wisdom to a different genre of viewers.

You can find Ruby on Instagram (@r.dhalwriter), Facebook (@r.dhalwriter), Tiktok (@r.dhalwriter), YouTube (Ruby Dhal) and Twitter (@rdhalwriter).

Ruby also holds healing sessions via phone, skype and email, as well as mentoring sessions and workshops. You can find all the relevant information about the work Ruby does, as well as her blog on www.rubydhal.com.

CPSIA information can be obtained
at www.ICGtesting.com
Printed in the USA
LVHW091931160221
679324LV00002B/112